3

## What are Oxford Literature Companions?

Oxford Literature Companions is a series designed to provide you with comprehensive support for popular set texts. You can use the Companion alongside your play, using relevant sections during your studies or using the book as a whole for revision.

Each Companion includes detailed guidance and practical activities on:

- Plot and Structure
- Context
- Characters
- Language
- Themes
- Performance
- Skills and Practice

## How does this book help with exam preparation?

As well as providing guidance on key areas of the play, throughout this book you will also find 'Upgrade' features. These are tips to help with your exam preparation and performance.

In addition, in the extensive **Skills and Practice** chapter, the Preparing for your assessment section provides detailed guidance on areas such as how to prepare for the exam, understanding the question, planning your response and hints for what to do (or not do) in the exam.

In the **Skills and Practice** chapter there is also a bank of **Sample questions** and **Sample answers**. The **Sample answers** are marked and include annotations and a summative comment.

## How does this book help with terminology?

Throughout the book, key terms are **highlighted** in the text and explained on the same page. There is also a detailed **Glossary** at the end of the book that explains, in the context of the play, all the relevant literary terms highlighted in this book.

## Which edition of the play has this book used?

Quotations have been taken from the Oxford University Press edition of *Romeo & Juliet* (ISBN 978-0-19-832166-8)

# How does this book work?

Each book in the Oxford Literature Companions series follows the same approach and includes the following features:

- **Key quotations** from the play
- **Key terms** explained on the page and linked to a complete glossary at the end of the book
- **Activity boxes** to help improve your understanding of the text
- **Upgrade** tips to help prepare you for your assessment

To help illustrate the features in this book, here are two annotated pages taken from this Oxford Literature Companion:

**Key terms** explained on the page and at the end of the book

**Activity boxes** to help improve your understanding of the play

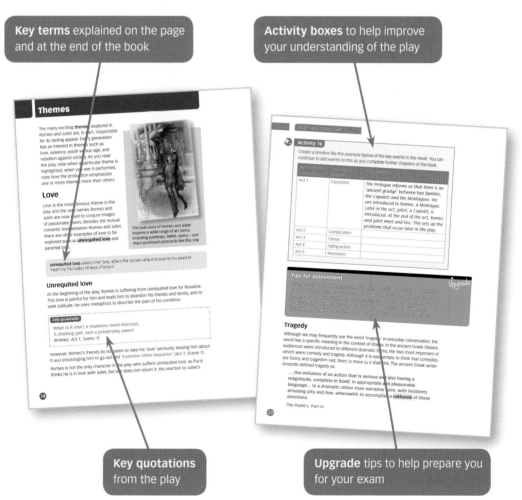

**Key quotations** from the play

**Upgrade** tips to help prepare you for your exam

## Plot

William Shakespeare's play *Romeo and Juliet* follows the romance between Romeo, a Montague, and Juliet, a Capulet, who fall in love despite being from rival families.

### The Prologue

The **Chorus** explains to the audience that there are two feuding families in Verona. Despite their 'ancient grudge', two of their children become 'star-cross'd lovers' and ultimately take their own lives. Only the death of the children ends the feud between the families.

- The **Prologue foreshadows** the ending of the play.
- It explains that the play is set in Verona, Italy and involves two families of equal status.
- It uses violent **imagery** to create a sense of excitement and anticipation.

> **Chorus** in Elizabethan drama, an actor who recites the Prologue and may comment at other times on the action of the play
>
> **foreshadowing** a literary device in which the author hints at what will happen at a later point
>
> **imagery** the use of visual or other vivid language to convey ideas or emotions
>
> **Prologue** in drama, an introductory scene, often written in verse, which establishes the themes, plot or characters of the play; from the Greek *pro* (before) and *logos* (word)

**Activity 1**

1. Read the Prologue aloud, emphasizing the violent words and images. Then read it again, this time emphasizing the positive ones. Explain which you think dominates this speech and why.

2. Experiment with different ways of presenting this speech to an audience, such as choral (group) speaking, narration accompanied by still images or a news reporter presenting a breaking news story. Discuss which do you think works best and why.

### Act 1, Scene 1

A quarrel breaks out between members of the Capulet and Montague households, starting with the servants but eventually including the most senior members of both families. Prince Escales stops the brawl and declares that if any more fighting 'disturb our streets' the troublemakers will be sentenced to death. Lady Montague asks Benvolio, Romeo's friend, where Romeo is and Benvolio describes Romeo's solitary and depressed behaviour. Benvolio seeks out Romeo and discovers that Romeo is in love with Rosaline, who has rejected him.

- Humour is created through the use of **puns** and word play, e.g. 'we'll not carry coals'/'colliers'/'choler'.
- The escalating violence in this scene captures the audience's attention.
- Romeo, one of the play's **protagonists**, is described to the audience before he is seen.

The Capulets and Montagues fight in this ballet production of Romeo & Juliet.

**Key quotations**

If ever you disturb our streets again,

Your lives shall pay the forfeit of the peace.

*(Prince Escales)*

 **Activity 2**

Why do you think Romeo was not involved in the street brawl? What do you learn about him from his father's and Benvolio's descriptions of his behaviour?

**protagonist** the main character

**pun** a type of joke or word play that relies on the similar sound but different meaning of words

## Act 1, Scene 2

Paris, a wealthy young man, approaches Lord Capulet, asking his permission to marry Juliet. Lord Capulet refuses, saying that she is too young – 'My child is yet a stranger in the world' – and suggesting that they wait two more years. He invites Paris to a feast he is holding that evening. Benvolio persuades Romeo to gatecrash the Capulet party as he will see Rosaline amongst 'all the admired beauties of Verona', who he will find more beautiful.

- This scene establishes Lord Capulet's great affection for his daughter when he says, 'She's the hopeful lady of my earth.'
- Romeo and Benvolio's playful natures are presented in the comic scene in which they trick a Capulet servant into revealing the details of the party.

> **Key quotations**
>
> My will to her consent is but a part
> *(Lord Capulet)*
>
> Compare her face with some that I shall show,
> And I will make thee think thy swan a crow.
> *(Benvolio)*

> **Activity 3**
>
> Re-read Lord Capulet's dialogue with Paris in this scene. Write a paragraph explaining what this shows about his feelings for Juliet.

## Act 1, Scene 3

Lady Capulet tells Juliet and her Nurse about Paris's marriage proposal. Lady Capulet describes 'valiant Paris' in glowing terms, making clear she feels he will be a good match for Juliet as he is very attractive and wealthy, 'So shall you share all that he doth possess'. She advises Juliet to observe Paris at the feast, suggesting that she will find herself able to love him. Juliet agrees to obey her parents' wishes.

- Lady Capulet appears to have a more distant relationship with her daughter as she asks the Nurse to stay and 'hear our counsel'.
- Lady Capulet's extravagant praise of Paris, using an extended simile to describe him as an expensive book, demonstrates her eagerness for Juliet to marry him.
- The Nurse is introduced as a talkative and humorous character, who is extremely fond of Juliet: 'Thou wast the prettiest babe that e'er I nurs'd'.

**Key quotations**

I'll look to like, if looking liking move;
But no more deep will I endart mine eye
Than your consent gives strength to make it fly.
*(Juliet)*

## Tips for assessment

In order to show understanding of structure, consider how characters are introduced in the play. In this scene, we see Juliet and the Nurse for the first time (Lady Capulet briefly appears in the first scene). Think about why Shakespeare did not choose to introduce them earlier in the play. What is the effect of their introduction in this scene?

## Act 1, Scene 4

A reluctant Romeo is persuaded by his friends Benvolio and Mercutio to enter the Capulets' party in disguise with them. Romeo has misgivings about going, as he thinks there is **'Some consequence yet hanging in the stars'**, but resigns himself to fate.

● Mercutio reveals his quick-witted and imaginative nature with his famous 'Queen Mab' speech.

Romeo and Juliet fall in love at first sight at the ball

**Key quotations**

But He that hath the steerage of my course
Direct my sail!
*(Romeo)*

## Act 1, Scene 5

Romeo sees Juliet and falls in love at first sight, saying **'For I ne'er saw true beauty till this night'**. Tybalt, Juliet's cousin, recognizes Romeo as a Montague but is stopped from attacking him by Lord Capulet. Romeo and Juliet meet and kiss. When Juliet leaves, Romeo discovers her identity. Juliet is told by her Nurse that Romeo is a Montague.

● Upon seeing Juliet, Romeo immediately forgets his former love Rosaline, which some view as a sign of his fickle or impulsive nature.

- Tybalt is presented as Romeo's **antagonist**.
- The religious imagery in Romeo and Juliet's shared **sonnet** suggests the strength and purity of their love.

> **Key quotations**
>
> Did my heart love till now? forswear it, sight!
> For I ne'er saw true beauty till this night.
> *(Romeo)*
>
> [...] If he be married,
> My grave is like to be my wedding bed.
> *(Juliet)*
>
> My only love sprung from my only hate!
> *(Juliet)*

**antagonist** a character who opposes the protagonist

**sonnet** a 14-line poem with a formal rhyme scheme and condensed form; often for expressing strong emotions, particularly love; in Shakespearean sonnets the rhyme scheme is ABABCDCDEFEFGG

**Activity 4**

Romeo and Juliet's meeting has changed how both characters feel about love. Write a diary entry from the point of view of either character, exploring how this unexpected meeting has made him or her feel. Remember to express any concerns the character may have about this relationship.

## Act 2, Scene 1

Benvolio and Mercutio leave the party looking for Romeo, who hides from them. Mercutio jokes about Romeo's love for Rosaline and his romantic nature.

- Romeo is behaving dangerously by not leaving with his friends.
- Romeo's romantic nature contrasts with Mercutio's more **ribald** and comic one, which is demonstrated by his use of puns such as 'pop'rin pear'.

## Act 2, Scene 2

Romeo hides in the orchard of Juliet's house. She appears on the balcony and, unaware that she is being overheard by Romeo, says that she wishes that Romeo was 'not a Montague' so that she could love him freely. Romeo speaks to her and confesses his **'heart's dear love'**. They arrange to marry and agree that Juliet's Nurse will act as their messenger.

- Juliet's unguarded declaration of love in her **soliloquy** accelerates the plot as Romeo is confident of his feelings being **reciprocated** and matches her passion.

- The scene combines both a delight in their mutual love and a sense of the danger into which they are entering.

> **reciprocate** to give something e.g. (love) in return; opposite of unrequited
>
> **ribald** crude or vulgar humour, usually involving jokes about sex
>
> **soliloquy** where a character voices aloud their innermost thoughts for the audience to hear

**Key quotations**

He jests at scars that never felt a wound.
But soft, what light through yonder window breaks?
It is the east, and Juliet is the sun.
*(Romeo)*

O Romeo, Romeo, wherefore art thou Romeo?
*(Juliet)*

**Activity 5**

This scene takes place in the Capulets' orchard at night.

1. Identify any quotations that stress that it is night time.

2. Now pick out any imagery linked with nature from the scene.

3. Write a paragraph explaining how both the imagery and setting help to create the drama of the scene.

# Act 2, Scene 3

Romeo seeks out Friar Lawrence to ask his advice. Although he believes that Romeo is acting impulsively, Friar Lawrence agrees to marry Romeo to Juliet.

- The scene begins with the Friar describing the medicinal herbs he has gathered, dwelling on the good and bad, or **'virtue'** and **'vice'**, that can be found in nature.

- The Friar's speech confirms his unusual ability to create medicines and potions, which becomes important in Act 4 and foreshadows how the good of Romeo and Juliet's love is swallowed up by the **'canker'** of the ancient feud.

- Friar Lawrence's condoning of the marriage is an important plot element.

> **Key quotations**
>
> In one respect I'll thy assistant be:
> For this alliance may so happy prove
> To turn your households' rancour to pure love.
> *(Friar Lawrence)*
>
> Wisely and slow, they stumble that run fast.
> *(Friar Lawrence)*

> **Activity 6**
>
> Re-read the ending of Act 2, Scene 3 from Friar Lawrence's line, 'Holy Saint Francis, what a change is here!' to the end of the scene. Pick out any quotations that suggest that Friar Lawrence believes that Romeo is not wise or sincere when it comes to love and contrast these with Romeo's replies to the Friar.

## Act 2, Scene 4

Benvolio reveals to Mercutio that Tybalt, nicknamed the 'Prince of Cats', has sent a challenge to Romeo's house. Mercutio teases Romeo about leaving them the night before, assuming that Romeo was with a woman. The Nurse arrives and is mocked by Mercutio. In secret, Romeo tells the Nurse to 'devise/ Some means' for Juliet to come to Friar Lawrence's cell to be married.

- Mercutio reveals his irreverent nature by ridiculing famous tragic lovers like Dido and Cleopatra and indulging in rude puns.
- This scene combines both the threat of Tybalt's challenge and the humour created by Mercutio and the Nurse.

> **Key quotations**
>
> A gentleman, Nurse, that loves to hear himself talk, and will speak more in a minute than he will stand to in a month. *(Romeo about Mercutio)*

## Act 2, Scene 5

Juliet waits impatiently for the Nurse to return with news from Romeo. The Nurse returns and eventually tells Juliet to go to Friar Lawrence's cell as she is to be married to Romeo on that day.

- Humour is established by the contrast between Juliet's urgent desire to know what the message from Romeo is and the Nurse's many complaints and efforts to keep her in suspense.
- The way the Nurse teases Juliet suggests the intimacy of their relationship.

## Act 2, Scene 6

Romeo and Juliet arrive at Friar Lawrence's cell to be married.

- Friar Lawrence expresses his unease at the marriage, **'These violent delights have violent ends'**, which foreshadows future events.

- Romeo and Juliet express their mutual joy and love.

Romeo and Juliet get married in Baz Luhrman's 1996 film, *William Shakespeare's Romeo + Juliet*, starring Leonardo DiCaprio and Claire Danes

> **Key quotations**
>
> **These violent delights have violent ends,**
> **And in their triumph die like fire and powder,**
> **Which as they kiss consume.**
> *(Friar Lawrence)*

 **Activity 7**

In this scene, Friar Lawrence expresses concern about the impending marriage and offers advice to Romeo.

1. Improvise an additional scene in which Friar Lawrence tries to persuade Romeo to be less impulsive and hasty.

2. Hot-seat the actors in role and ask questions to discover why Friar Lawrence is worried and why Romeo cannot wait or be cautious.

## Act 3, Scene 1

Tybalt, who is looking for Romeo, confronts Benvolio and Mercutio. When Romeo appears he refuses to fight with Tybalt. Outraged by Romeo's 'dishonourable, vile submission', Mercutio fights with Tybalt instead and is killed when Romeo attempts to stop the fight. The dying Mercutio curses both the Montagues and Capulets with the words, 'A plague a'both your houses!' To avenge Mercutio, Romeo kills Tybalt and runs away. Prince Escales exiles Romeo for the death of Tybalt.

- This scene is a turning point when the comic elements of the play are overtaken by tragedy.
- The setting of this scene is very important. Shakespeare states that it is a public place and there are references to it being warm, both of which add to the tension and high emotion in the scene.
- Romeo is torn between his love for Juliet (and by extension the Capulet family, including Tybalt) and his desire to avenge his friend's death. His impulsive nature means that he forgets the threat of banishment and allows 'fire-ey'd fury' to lead him to his destruction.

> **Key quotations**
>
> O calm, dishonourable, vile submission!
> *(Mercutio)*
>
> O, I am fortune's fool!
> *(Romeo)*
>
> [...] Let Romeo hence in haste,
> Else, when he is found, that hour is his last.
> *(Prince Escales)*

> **Activity 8**
>
> This scene is a turning point for the character of Romeo. Write a paragraph explaining how he transforms so quickly from peacemaker to murderer.

## Act 3, Scene 2

Unaware that Romeo has been involved in a violent brawl, Juliet eagerly awaits his arrival in anticipation of spending their wedding night together: 'Romeo/ Leap to these arms'. The Nurse brings Juliet the bad news that Romeo has slain Tybalt and is now banished. The Nurse agrees to find Romeo and to bring him to Juliet that night.

- Juliet, in eager and lusty anticipation of her wedding night – 'Gallop apace, you fiery-footed steeds', changes to a more sober realization of their inevitable separation with the repetition of the words 'death', 'woe' and 'banished'.

- This scene mirrors aspects of Act 2, Scene 5 as both involve Juliet awaiting news that is clumsily delivered by the Nurse.

> **Key quotations**
>
> O, I have bought the mansion of a love,
> But not possess'd it, and though I am sold,
> Not yet enjoy'd.
> *(Juliet)*

**Activity 9**

Juliet experiences a range of emotions in this scene, from joyful anticipation to the greatest despair. Create a graph charting her emotional state, adding quotations from the scene to show her changing emotions.

## Act 3, Scene 3

Friar Lawrence tries to persuade Romeo to accept his banishment. The Nurse arrives and describes Juliet's despair. Romeo threatens to kill himself but is stopped by the Nurse. Friar Lawrence scolds him for his behaviour and encourages him to look at his many blessings. The Nurse gives Romeo the ring sent by Juliet and he arranges to see Juliet before going to Mantua under Friar Lawrence's guidance.

- Friar Lawrence offers a philosophy to encourage Romeo to accept his banishment, as well as making practical arrangements for them to remain in contact during the banishment.
- Romeo's extreme emotional state is emphasized by his equating of banishment with death and his apparent willingness to kill himself.
- Friar Lawrence's more positive approach to the crisis is emphasized by his repetition of positive words like 'love'.

> **Key quotations**
>
> Ha, banishment? be merciful, say 'death'
> *(Romeo)*
>
> [...] Heaven is here
> Where Juliet lives
> *(Romeo)*

**Tips for assessment**

Friar Lawrence is very important to the plot of the play. If asked about his role, consider when he intervenes in the action of the play and what the outcome is.

## Act 3, Scene 4

In a late evening discussion, Paris persuades Lord and Lady Capulet to 'commend me to your daughter' and that it is the right time for him to marry Juliet. Lord Capulet changes his mind about Juliet being too young to marry and agrees 'She shall be married to this noble earl.'

- Tybalt's death has made Lord Capulet aware of mortality – 'we were born to die' – perhaps prompting his change of heart.
- Lord Capulet believes that Juliet will obey his wishes.

> **Key quotations**
>
> [...] I think she will be rul'd
> In all respects by me
> *(Lord Capulet)*

**Activity 10**

Explore how Lord Capulet's attitude to Juliet marrying Paris changes between Act 1, Scene 2 and Act 3, Scene 4. Compare his views on:

- Juliet's readiness to be married
- Juliet's ability to choose her own husband
- When Juliet should be married

## Act 3, Scene 5

After spending the night together, Romeo and Juliet part, with Romeo promising that they will meet again. Juliet is weeping when her mother arrives to tell her that she is to be married to Paris as his 'joyful bride'. When Juliet refuses, her father is furious and threatens to disown her. In private, the Nurse tells Juliet she should marry Paris, even though she is already married to Romeo.

- There is **dramatic irony** in this scene as the audience knows the true cause of Juliet's tears but her mother does not.
- Juliet's previous relationships with both the Nurse and her father dramatically

Juliet infuriates her parents when she refuses to marry Paris.

change in this scene. She no longer confides in the Nurse, and her father, who once seemed to dote on her, is now seen as a cruel and violent figure.

- This is the last time Juliet sees Romeo alive. Their tender farewells evoke feelings of **pathos** in the audience.

> **dramatic Irony** when the words or action of a scene are understood by the audience but not by one or more of the characters on stage. For example, when Juliet says **'Ay, madam, from the reach of these my hands./Would none but I might venge my cousin's death!'**, her mother believes that Juliet wishes she could kill Romeo, whereas the audience understands that she wishes to protect him
>
> **pathos** something that creates feelings of sympathy and pity

**Key quotations**

It was the nightingale, and not the lark
*(Juliet)*

Marry, my child, early next Thursday morn,
The gallant, young, and noble gentleman,
The County Paris, at Saint Peter's Church
Shall happily make thee there a joyful bride.
*(Lady Capulet)*

I would the fool were married to her grave.
*(Lady Capulet)*

Hang thee, young baggage, disobedient wretch!
*(Lord Capulet)*

> **Activity 11**
>
> Compare the language Lord Capulet uses towards Juliet in this scene with his description of her in Act 1, Scene 2. Make a list of the reasons why he behaves in this way.

## Act 4, Scene 1

Paris meets with Friar Lawrence to arrange his marriage to Juliet. Juliet comes to confide in Friar Lawrence, briefly speaking with Paris before he leaves. Juliet tells Friar Lawrence that she would rather die than marry Paris. Friar Lawrence explains his plan to give her a potion to make it appear as if she is dead and then allow her to join Romeo in Mantua.

- Once again Friar Lawrence's importance to the plot is established, not only with his plan to make it appear that Juliet has died but also with his promise to send Romeo a letter informing him of their scheme.
- The tense conversation between Paris and Juliet is another example of dramatic irony, as the audience understands the reasons for Juliet's rejection of Paris far better than he does.

> **Key quotations**
>
> Be not so long to speak, I long to die,
> If what thou speak'st speak not of remedy.
> *(Juliet)*

> **Activity 12**
>
> Re-read Juliet's speech from 'O bid me leap' to 'To live an unstain'd wife to my sweet love'. Look at the language Juliet uses to express the strength of her emotions and identify any imagery that foreshadows the ending of the play.

## Act 4, Scene 2

Juliet returns home and asks her father's forgiveness, vowing 'Henceforward I am ever rul'd by you'. Lord Capulet enthusiastically moves the wedding date forward to Wednesday, despite his wife's objections.

- Juliet disguises her real feelings and plays the role of obedient daughter.
- Capulet's statement that 'All our whole city is much bound to' Friar Lawrence is ironic given his role in Juliet's deception.

**Tips for assessment**

Juliet disguises her true feelings in this scene. In your assessment, make sure you are clear about when characters are saying what they really think and when they are hiding their thoughts and feelings.

## Act 4, Scene 3

After dismissing her mother and her Nurse, Juliet is left alone to contemplate her 'hideous fears' of taking the potion that the Friar has provided for her. In the end, she drinks it.

- Juliet's isolation is emphasized by her fear that even Friar Lawrence may be trying to trick her into taking poison to hide his role in her marriage to Romeo.
- She uses vivid imagery in her soliloquy to conjure her nightmare vision of being trapped alive in a tomb.

**Key quotations**

I have a faint cold fear thrills through my veins
That almost freezes up the heat of life:
I'll call them back again to comfort me.
Nurse! – What should she do here?
My dismal scene I needs must act alone.
*(Juliet)*

**Activity 13**

In this scene, Juliet must decide whether or not to drink the potion.

1. Create a conscience alley. One person in the role of Juliet should walk down the alley, listening to the reasons why she should drink the potion and the reasons why she shouldn't.

2. Write a paragraph describing Juliet's doubts, supporting them with examples from the text. Remember to explain why she does eventually drink the potion.

## Act 4, Scene 4

The next morning, Lord and Lady Capulet make excited arrangements for the wedding. Capulet merrily orders the servants to get busy preparing for the feast and asks the Nurse to 'Go waken Juliet'.

- Capulet appears light-hearted as the preparations for Juliet's wedding proceed. This contrasts with the violent threats he issued in Act 3, Scene 5.

## Act 4, Scene 5

The Capulets' wedding plans are interrupted when they discover that Juliet cannot be awakened. Her 'death' is mourned and the wedding arrangements are changed to those for a funeral.

- Different members of the Capulet household demonstrate their despair at Juliet's death.
- Friar Lawrence attempts to comfort them by saying that 'heaven hath all'.

### Tips for assessment

In your assessment, you may be asked to comment on the structure of the play. One aspect of structure is the relationship of scenes to each other, e.g. the contrast between the light-hearted and hopeful preparations for Juliet's wedding in Act 4, Scene 4 and the sudden and dramatic mourning for Juliet's supposed 'death' in Act 4, Scene 5.

## Act 5, Scene 1

In Mantua, Romeo receives news from his servant Balthasar that Juliet is dead. Romeo goes to an apothecary to buy some poison to kill himself.

- Romeo's opening soliloquy about his dream, when he says 'I dreamt my lady came and found me dead', ironically foreshadows later events.
- Once again Romeo acts impulsively, which contributes to the tragic outcome of the play.

---

**Key quotations**

Put this in any liquid thing you will
And drink it off, and if you had the strength
Of twenty men, it would dispatch you straight.
(Apothecary)

---

## Act 5, Scene 2

Friar John informs Friar Lawrence that he was unable to deliver the letter about the plan to Romeo. Friar Lawrence decides to go to the tomb alone in order to be there when Juliet awakens.

- The unfortunate coincidence of a suspected **plague** preventing the delivery of the letter to Romeo in Mantua is an important plot point.

> **plague** the Bubonic Plague or 'Black Death', a deadly infectious disease which was rapidly spread by infected people and animals

## Act 5, Scene 3

Paris comes to the churchyard to mourn Juliet's death and spies Romeo arriving, ready to break into the tomb in order to be with Juliet. Paris confronts the 'vile Montague', they fight and Romeo kills Paris. Romeo enters the tomb, embraces and kisses Juliet, then drinks the poison. Awakening, Juliet discovers that Romeo is dead. She takes his dagger and kills herself. Arriving at the tomb, the Prince questions Friar Lawrence, Balthasar and Paris's page to determine the sequence

Juliet is distraught to find on awakening that Romeo is dead and takes his dagger to kill herself.

of these tragic events. He chastises the Capulet and Montague familes: 'See what a scourge is laid upon your hate'. The feuding families are united by the death of their children.

- Paris's affection for Juliet is revealed by both his mourning and his dying request for Romeo to 'Open the tomb, lay me with Juliet.'
- When commenting on Juliet's beauty, Romeo ironically notes that death has not affected her: 'Death [...]/ Hath had no power yet upon thy beauty'.
- Both Romeo and Juliet end their farewell speeches to each other with a kiss.

> **Key quotations**
>
> Come, bitter conduct, come, unsavoury guide!
> Thou desperate pilot, now at once run on
> The dashing rocks thy seasick weary bark!
> Here's to my love! [*Drinks*] O true apothecary!
> Thy drugs are quick. Thus with a kiss I die.
> *(Romeo)*
>
> For never was a story of more woe
> Than this of Juliet and her Romeo.
> *(Prince Escales)*

**Activity 14**

As a director, how would you stage the ending of the play to reinforce the reconciliation between the families? Create a series of still images showing your staging ideas for the section beginning with the Prince's line, 'Capulet, Montague?/ See what a scourge is laid upon your hate', to the end of the scene.

# Structure

## Handling of time

Time is mentioned throughout the play, from the Chorus's promise that the play will occupy 'the two hours' traffic of our stage' *(The Prologue)* to the Prince's reminder of the time of day with the 'glooming peace' of the morning in his final speech in Act 5, Scene 3. Given the many events of the play – falling in love, marrying, deaths, banishment, a second engagement, more deaths – it may be surprising to learn that the action of the play takes only four days.

In some scenes, Shakespeare is very precise about when events occur; e.g. in Act 3, Scene 4, Capulet asks what day it is and is told it is Monday. Capulet then arranges for Paris to marry Juliet on Thursday, but in his excitement in Act 4, Scene 2 changes the date for the marriage to Wednesday. When Juliet discovers that Romeo has been banished, she notes that she is his 'three-hours' wife' *(Act 3, Scene 2)*.

The characters' reactions to time create tension and propel the **tragedy**. Some characters rush ahead of time, e.g. Juliet impatiently wishing for night so she can be with Romeo in Act 3, Scene 2, and others want to slow it down, as Friar Lawrence does by warning, 'Wisely and slow, they stumble that run fast' in Act 2, Scene 3.

**tragedy** a play in which the main character, usually a man of high status, is brought down through a combination of his own personal weaknesses and factors beyond his control, such as fate

**Activity 15**

1. Create a chart with Sunday, Monday, Tuesday and Wednesday written down the left-hand side. Detail the events that occur on each day, using brightly coloured pens to mark positive, happy, comic or romantic events and darker colours to indicate tragic events such as deaths.

2. Write a paragraph explaining why Shakespeare may have chosen to condense so much action into so little time.

## Five-act structure

*Romeo and Juliet* is written in five acts. The five-act structure first became popular during Roman times and was revived by Renaissance playwrights. The German writer Gustav Freytag (1816–1895) analysed the five-act structure as summarized below:

- **Act 1: Exposition** The setting is established and the characters introduced. Background information may be supplied and possible sources of conflict suggested.

- **Act 2: Complications** Conflicts occur and problems are presented. Events begin to accelerate (which is referred to as 'rising action').

- **Act 3: Climax** The development of conflict reaches its high point. There may be a turning point where the protagonist must make a choice that affects the outcome of the play.

- **Act 4: Falling action** The consequences of Act 3 are felt, momentum slows and tension is heightened by false hopes and fear. In a tragedy, it looks, at least momentarily, as if the protagonist can succeed.

- **Act 5: Resolution** The conflict is resolved, whether through a catastrophe such as the downfall or death of the protagonist, or through his or her victory.

## Activity 16

Create a timeline like the example below of the key events in the novel. You can continue to add events to this as you complete further chapters of the book.

| Act of *Romeo and Juliet* | Structural purpose | Explanation |
|---|---|---|
| Act 1 | Exposition | The Prologue informs us that there is an 'ancient grudge' between two families, the Capulets and the Montagues. We are introduced to Romeo, a Montague. Later in the act, Juliet, a Capulet, is introduced. At the end of the act, Romeo and Juliet meet and kiss. This sets up the problems that occur later in the play. |
| Act 2 | Complication | |
| Act 3 | Climax | |
| Act 4 | Falling action | |
| Act 5 | Resolution | |

### Tips for assessment

When writing about the structure of *Romeo and Juliet*, remember that it is a play and has a different form to a novel, poem or short story. For example, remember to write about acts and scenes rather than chapters. You won't be discussing the narrator or narrative voice, but instead will look at techniques like dialogue, soliloquies, monologues and stage directions.

## Tragedy

Although we may frequently use the word 'tragedy' in everyday conversation, the word has a specific meaning in the context of drama. In the ancient Greek theatre, audiences were introduced to different dramatic forms, the two most important of which were comedy and tragedy. Although it is easy simply to think that comedies are funny and tragedies sad, there is more to it than this. The ancient Greek writer Aristotle defined tragedy as:

> ... the imitation of an action that is serious and also having a magnitude, complete in itself; in appropriate and pleasurable language... in a dramatic rather than narrative form; with incidents arousing pity and fear, wherewith to accomplish a **catharsis** of these emotions.

*The Poetics,* Part VI

The romance and tragedy are evident in this final scene from a ballet production of *Romeo and Juliet*

The word 'magnitude' suggests that the actions and characters are important and what we would think of as 'larger than life'. The characters are usually high born, in positions of power, such as King Oedipus in the Greek tragedy *Oedipus Rex*. They speak well ('appropriate and pleasurable language') and undergo upsetting and catastrophic events ('incidents arousing pity and fear'). The ancient Greek audience should feel cleansed and relieved at the end ('to accomplish a catharsis of these emotions').

Tragedies, with some alterations, were also popular in Elizabethan times and Shakespeare's plays are generally divided into tragedies, comedies and histories (which, as the name suggests, are plays based on Shakespeare's interpretation of real historical events). *Romeo and Juliet* is considered a tragedy and the earliest of these plays to be written and performed; the other tragedies include *Hamlet*, *Macbeth* and *Othello*. Although there are many elements of comedy (an exotic location, disguises, word play and puns) in the first two acts of *Romeo and Juliet*, the events following Mercutio's death firmly establish it as a tragedy. Typical components of Shakespearean tragedy include:

- a tragic hero of high status
- a **tragic flaw** in the character of the tragic hero
- a plot involving the downfall of the hero
- the death of the tragic hero
- a restoring of order.

**catharsis** the purification or cleansing of emotion

**tragic flaw** a defect or failing in the tragic protagonist that brings around his downfall, e.g. Macbeth's ambition or Othello's jealousy

*Romeo and Juliet* differs a little from this in that, like *Antony and Cleopatra* (another romantic Shakespearean tragedy), there are potentially two tragic heroes. At first reading, it may seem that Romeo is the play's protagonist. After all, he is introduced to the audience before Juliet and his tragic flaw of impulsiveness is suggested by his willingness to fall so quickly out of love with Rosaline and into love with Juliet. The Shakespearean critic, William Hazlitt wrote 'Romeo is Hamlet in love.' However, others believe that the play belongs to Juliet, whose role is one of the longest ever written by Shakespeare for a female character. Juliet is a deep and well-rounded character whose biography is fleshed out by the details of her childhood supplied by the Nurse and, as the play progresses, the difficulty of her choices is played out for the audience, particularly in her moving speech in Act 4, Scene 3. While the play begins with Romeo receiving first billing in the title, it ends with 'Juliet and her Romeo'. Whether you believe that they are both tragic heroes or that the plot follows one more than the other, the tragic arc of the play, including their deaths and the restoring of order through the reconciliation between the Montagues and Capulets, is clear.

## Activity 17

In *Tragedy: A Very Short Introduction* (OUP, 2005), Adrian Poole writes:

> Yet in a broad sense, tragedy always deals with toxic matter bequeathed by the past to the present. In personal terms, this often means what fathers and mothers have passed on to their children in the form of duties, loyalties, passions and injuries.

Discuss this idea with a partner and decide if it applies to the plot of *Romeo and Juliet*. Write a paragraph explaining how the plot of *Romeo and Juliet* fits this definition of a tragedy.

# Writing about plot and structure

*Upgrade*

In your assessment, it is important that you demonstrate understanding of the whole play, not just a section of it. Even if you are only required to write about a given scene or extract, you must understand the context of the scene in order to demonstrate insight.

Never just retell the story of the play. Instead, make sure that you are able to select key moments or explain how one event leads to another.

In order to improve your writing about plot and structure, practise the following:

- Identify key moments in the play such as turning points, climaxes or resolutions.
- Show an understanding of the conventions of the tragic form.
- Consider when in the play an event has happened and if it has an impact on later events.
- Consider how Shakespeare's handling of time increases the tension and suspense of the play.
- Reflect on the impact of certain events or lines because of techniques like foreshadowing.
- Remember that this is a play performed in front of audiences, so refer to the audience rather than the reader.

## Biography of William Shakespeare

Shakespeare (1564–1616) is thought to have written *Romeo and Juliet* in 1596

- Shakespeare was born in 1564, when Queen Elizabeth I was queen of England.
- He is believed to have studied at a grammar school in Stratford-upon-Avon, where he would have been taught subjects such as Latin and rhetoric. Like most young people of that time, he did not go to university.
- He married Anne Hathaway and they had three children: Susanna, and twins, Hamnet and Judith.
- By 1592, he was working as an actor and playwright in London.
- The plays he wrote between 1594 and 1599 included *A Midsummer Night's Dream* and *Romeo and Juliet*.
- His son Hamnet died in 1596, the year *Romeo and Juliet* is thought to have been written.
- Many of his greatest tragedies, such as *Hamlet*, *Othello* and *King Lear*, were written in the period between 1599 and 1608.
- He died in 1616 and was buried in Stratford-upon-Avon.

## Historical and cultural context

### The historical period

The Elizabethan Age (1558–1603) was a time when England was forging its identity. Signs of the country's confidence are found in its foreign adventures, growing wealth and creative output in literature, music and art. Along with the new queen, came the newly created Church of England, signalling the change from Catholic to Protestant beliefs.

It was also a time of great contrasts and contradictions. The great plays of Shakespeare were performed alongside the brutal **bear-baiting** pits of Southwark (there was a 'bear-garden,' an arena where the sport took place, near the Globe Theatre). Men were dominant and a woman could legally be beaten by her husband, yet the country was ruled by a brilliant woman, Elizabeth I. A rapidly growing London benefitted from increasing wealth from foreign trade but also suffered through the plague.

Besides Shakespeare, important writers from this period include the playwrights Christopher Marlowe (*Doctor Faustus*) and Ben Jonson (*Volpone*) and the poet Edmund Spenser ('The Faerie Queene').

**bear-baiting** a popular Elizabethan sport where hunting dogs attacked a chained bear, usually resulting in the death of many of the animals involved

# Sources for *Romeo and Juliet*

Like other playwrights of his time, Shakespeare would borrow plots from a variety of sources: history, fables, poetry and other plays. The story of Romeo and Juliet was a popular one and would have been known to many in the Elizabethan audience. For Shakespeare's play, the main source was Arthur Brooke's poem 'The Tragicall History of Romeus and Juliet', which was published in 1562. There are enough similarities between Shakespeare's play and the poem to make many scholars believe that Shakespeare kept a copy of the poem with him as he wrote the play. The two disputing households, the Verona setting, the masked ball, the deaths in the tomb and other key events occur in both. However there are also significant differences such as Juliet's age, which Shakespeare lowers from Brooke's 16 to 13, and the length of time of the action, which takes place over a number of months in the poem but only four days in the play.

## Activity 1

1.  Read the following extract from Arthur Brooke's introduction to 'The Tragicall History of Romeus and Juliet'. What similarities and differences can you find with the play *Romeo and Juliet*?

    > To this good end serve all ill ends of ill beginnings. And to this end, good Reader, is this tragical matter written, to describe unto thee a couple of unfortunate lovers, thralling themselves to unhonest desire; neglecting the authority and advice of parents and friends; conferring their principal counsels with drunken gossips and superstitious friars (the naturally fit instruments of unchastity); attempting all adventures of peril for th'attaining of their wished lust; using auricular confession the key of whoredom and treason, for furtherance of their purpose; abusing the honourable name of lawful marriage to cloak the shame of stolen contracts; finally by all means of unhonest life hasting to most unhappy death.

2.  In this introduction, Brooke seems to be criticizing the lovers. Do you believe this was Shakespeare's purpose in writing his play? Discuss your ideas.

# Marriage in Elizabethan times

Although the attitudes to marriage in *Romeo and Juliet* may seem surprising to us, given Juliet's youth and her parents' determination that she marry a man she barely knows, this would have been less shocking in Shakespeare's time. In *Elizabeth's London*, Liza Picard writes, 'Marriage involved a change of status. The woman moved from the power and responsibility of her father, to that of her husband… No marriage was binding if the parties were under age – fourteen for a boy and twelve for a girl.' Lady Capulet reveals to Juliet, **'I was your mother much upon these years / That you are now a maid'**. *(Lady Capulet, Act 1, Scene 3)*

> ### Activity 2
>
> In the opening section of Act 1, Scene 2, Capulet and Paris discuss Paris's desire to marry Juliet. Re-read their dialogue and make notes on anything you find surprising given Lady Capulet's opinion and Lord Capulet's actions in Act 3, Scene 5.

# Similarities to *A Midsummer Night's Dream*

Shakespeare wrote *Romeo and Juliet* and *A Midsummer Night's Dream* during the same time period and they bear many striking similarities. Both Juliet and Hermia wish to marry against the wishes of their families and each hopes to escape from the rules of society by fleeing with her lover. Both plays take place in the summer over a brief time period (Theseus begins *A Midsummer Night's Dream* declaring 'our nuptial hour draws on apace. Four happy days bring in another moon…').

While the marriage of Theseus and Hippolyta becomes a triple wedding for the couples in *A Midsummer Night's Dream*, the wedding in *Romeo and Juliet* transforms into a funeral. *A Midsummer Night's Dream* could be said to begin like a tragedy, with the threatened execution of Hermia, while *Romeo and Juliet* has many comic elements (puns, disguises, comic characters) but, with the deaths of Mercutio and Tybalt, turns tragic.

A fourteenth-century woodcut showing Thisbe driving Pyramus' sword through her heart

Fairies, dreams and the supernatural feature in both, especially in the portrayal of Puck in one and Mercutio's Queen Mab speech in the other. The final act of *A Midsummer Night's Dream* contains a play-within-a-play in which the 'mechanicals' perform a version of 'Pyramus and Thisbe' (based on a tale from Ovid's *Metamorphoses*), which bears an uncanny resemblance to the plot of *Romeo and Juliet*, although played for laughs.

## Activity 3

Read Thisbe's final speech below from the play-within-a-play in *A Midsummer Night's Dream*.

> **Key quotations**
>
> Asleep, my love?
> What, dead, my dove?
> O Pyramus, arise!
> Speak, speak. Quite dumb?
> Dead, dead? A tomb
> Must cover thy sweet eyes.
> These lily lips,
> This cherry nose,
> These yellow cowslip cheeks,
> Are gone, are gone:
> Lovers, make moan:
> His eyes were green as leeks.
> O Sisters Three,
> Come, come to me,
> With hands as pale as milk;
> Lay them in gore,
> Since you have shore
> With shears his thread of silk.
> Tongue, not a word:
> Come, trusty sword;
> Come, blade, my breast imbrue:
> *[Stabs herself]*
>
> And, farewell, friends;
> Thus Thisby ends:
> Adieu, adieu, adieu.
> *(Thisbe, A Midsummer's Night Dream)*

a) Compare the above speech with Juliet's speech from Act 5, Scene 3, beginning 'Go get thee hence...' to the line, '... there rust, and let me die.'

b) Discuss what aspects of romantic drama Shakespeare is **parodying** in this scene and how it differs from Juliet's death.

**parody** to mock or make fun of something by imitating it

# Religion and other beliefs

Religion was present in almost every aspect of Elizabethan life and people could be punished for holding what were considered to be the wrong beliefs. As a Christian society, the Elizabethan audience would have believed in the sanctity of marriage and the sinfulness of murder. Shakespeare set *Romeo and Juliet* in Italy, and the Capulets and Montagues are Catholic. This is emphasized by Juliet's and Romeo's reliance on the advice they receive from Friar Lawrence. Despite her passions, Juliet does not spend the night with Romeo until they are married and the Friar will not leave them unsupervised **'Till Holy Church incorporate two in one'** *(Act 2, Scene 6)*. When the Nurse suggests that Juliet forgets Romeo and undertakes a bigamous marriage with Paris, Juliet is shocked not only by the betrayal to Romeo but also because it would go against her Christian beliefs as she cannot marry again **'... Unless that husband send it me from heaven/ By leaving earth'** *(Act 3, Scene 5)*.

Typically, Lady Fortune is depicted here with the Wheel of Fortune, controlling the fate of her hapless victims

Perhaps more surprising, given Elizabethan sanctions against suicide, is how sympathetically the two characters' suicides are treated. Whereas, in the play *Hamlet*, Hamlet regrets that God has 'fix'd his canon 'gainst self-slaughter' so he cannot commit suicide without risking everlasting damnation, no such anxieties plague Romeo and Juliet. Professor René Weis argues that Shakespeare is 'bending the rules with his lovers' as 'young love triumphs, it seems, unconditionally in the teeth of doctrinal sanctions against self-murder'. Rather than being buried in unconsecrated ground, as would have been expected for suicides in Elizabethan times, their parents promise to erect golden statues to them and they will lie side by side.

Many Elizabethans also held other beliefs. For example, some felt that destiny was controlled by a Wheel of Fortune in which an individual's fortunes might rise or fall like the turn of the wheel.

Others put their faith in astrology, believing that the zodiac controlled their lives. People were judged to have been born under a lucky or an unlucky star and some would consult with astrologers before making plans. Shakespeare enters into the debate about the wisdom of believing in the stars in several of his plays; for example, in *Julius Caesar*, Cassius admonishes Brutus, saying 'The fault, dear Brutus, is not in the stars, but in ourselves.' However, in the Prologue of *Romeo and Juliet*, the lovers are identified as 'star-cross'd', suggesting that astrology had determined the outcome of their romance as unhappy.

Other Elizabethans believed in the importance of dreams, feeling that if they could unlock the secrets of their dreams they would be able to foretell the future. In Act 5, Scene 1, Romeo is presented as clearly believing this when he exclaims 'My dreams presage some joyful news at hand' although ironically he has misread his dream and does not realize that it foretells his own death. There were also those, like Cassius from *Julius Caesar*, who believed that, 'Men at some time are masters of their fates' and therefore responsible for their destinies.

## Activity 4

Read the following quotations and for each one discuss what we learn about the beliefs of the speaker.

1. 'True, I talk of dreams/ Which are the children of an idle brain,/ Begot of nothing but vain fantasy' *(Mercutio, Act 1, Scene 4)*

2. 'Some consequence yet hanging in the stars' *(Romeo, Act 1, Scene 4)*

3. 'O Fortune, Fortune, all men call thee fickle' *(Juliet, Act 3, Scene 5)*

4. 'Capulet, Montague?/ See what a scourge is laid upon your hate,/ That heaven finds means to kill your joys with love!' *(Prince, Act 5, Scene 3)*

## Writing about context

*Upgrade*

It is important to be aware if your assessment requires explicit reference to the context of *Romeo and Juliet*. If context is required, the examiner will not be looking simply for dates or unrelated historic facts. Instead, try to explain how the context gives you a greater insight into the play and how it can be interpreted in a way that is relevant to the question you are answering. Further information about context is provided in the Performance section on pages 68–77.

# Characters

## Main characters

### Romeo

Romeo is the only son of Lord and Lady Montague and, with Juliet, one of the play's protagonists. When first introduced to the audience, he is a moody and lovelorn boy who has been rejected by Rosaline. When his friends Benvolio and Mercutio persuade him to gatecrash the Capulet party, Romeo falls in love at first sight with Juliet, and she returns his love.

> **Key quotations**
>
> Did my heart love till now? forswear it, sight!
> For I ne'er saw true beauty till this night.
> *(Romeo, Act 1, Scene 5)*

With the joy of reciprocal love, Romeo distances himself from the teasing and brawling of his friends, seemingly confirming the earlier description of him as 'a virtuous and well-governed youth' *(Act 1, Scene 5)*. He refuses to fight Tybalt, Juliet's cousin, as they are now related by marriage, but, by doing so, unintentionally causes the death of Mercutio. His subsequent action, killing Tybalt in revenge, illustrates the contradictions in Romeo's character as he swiftly turns from peacemaker to murderer. While his impulsive actions may be the catalyst for the tragedy, he seems to view himself as a victim of fate.

> **Key quotations**
>
> O, I am fortune's fool.
> *(Romeo, Act 3, Scene 1)*

> **Activity 1**
>
> Read the following quotations from Romeo.
>
> But He that hath the steerage of my course/ Direct my sail!
> *(Act 1, Scene 4)*
>
> Is it e'en so? Then I defy you, stars! *(Act 5, Scene 1)*
>
> O give me thy hand,/ One writ with me in sour misfortune's book!
> *(Act 5, Scene 3)*
>
> Write a paragraph summarizing Romeo's attitude towards fate and fortune, and explain what this reveals about his character.

His passionate nature makes Romeo an exciting and appealing character, but his extreme reactions are demonstrated by his hasty marriage to Juliet and his determination to kill himself upon hearing of his banishment and later of Juliet's supposed death. Believing Juliet is dead, Romeo rushes to her tomb, killing Paris on the way, and then poisons himself before Juliet awakens. Despite his flaws and contradictions, he remains a symbol of uncompromising, youthful romantic love.

> **Key quotations**
>
> Call me but love, and I'll be new baptis'd;
> Henceforth I never will be Romeo.
> *(Romeo, Act 2, Scene 2)*
>
> I do protest I never injuried thee,
> But love thee better than thou canst devise
> *(Romeo, Act 3, Scene 1)*
>
> Thus with a kiss I die.
> *(Romeo, Act 5, Scene 3)*

**Activity 2**

Make a list of every occasion in the play when Romeo acts impulsively. Discuss whether or not you believe his impulsiveness causes his downfall.

## Juliet

Juliet is one of Shakespeare's most loved and challenging female characters. Her role is the second longest in the play (after Romeo's) and the third longest female Shakespearean character written (after Cleopatra in *Antony and Cleopatra* and Rosalind in *As You Like It*). Surprisingly, she is not described physically and we do not know if she is blonde or dark, tall or short. We learn that she is the 13-year-old only daughter of the Capulet household and she is first presented as a sheltered and obedient girl, who is willing to be guided by her family in her choice of husband.

> **Key quotations**
>
> But no more deep will I endart mine eye
> Than your consent gives strength to make it fly.
> *(Juliet, Act 1, Scene 3)*

Upon meeting Romeo, she passionately reciprocates his love and frequently takes the lead in their relationship, at times, unwittingly, as when she declares her love for him without knowing she is being overheard in Act 2, Scene 2. When Romeo offers **clichéd** images of love, she corrects him, encouraging him to be more truthful and original. It is Juliet who first mentions marriage, insistent that Romeo's intentions should be 'honourable'.

**Key quotations**

What's in a name? That which we call a rose
By any other word would smell as sweet
*(Juliet, Act 2, Scene 2)*

**clichéd** unoriginal and over-used

Juliet takes matters into her own hands by drinking the sleeping potion and, in this scene of Olivia Hussey from Franco Zeffirelli's 1968 film, by plunging Romeo's dagger into her heart

**Activity 3**

One way to explore a character is to analyse what other characters say about them. Use a chart like the one below to record this information and explain what this suggests about Juliet.

| Act | What other characters say about Juliet |
|-----|----------------------------------------|
| Act 1 | 'My child is yet a stranger to the world' *(Capulet, Act 1, Scene 2)*: this suggests that Juliet is naïve and inexperienced. |
| Act 2 | |
| Act 3 | |
| Act 4 | |
| Act 5 | |

Juliet's 'Gallop apace' speech in Act 3, Scene 2 was considered shocking by some audiences as it shows her sensual and passionate nature when she yearns for her wedding night. After Romeo's banishment and dreading the proposed hasty marriage to Paris, Juliet finds herself increasingly isolated. She refuses to submit to her parents' wishes for her marriage to Paris and bears her father's subsequent anger. As she feels she can no longer trust her Nurse, she relies on the advice of Friar Lawrence and bravely drinks the potion which she hopes will lead to the possibility of being reunited with Romeo. Hers is the final death in the play.

My dismal scene I needs must act alone.
*(Juliet, Act 4, Scene 3)*

**Activity 4**

Write a paragraph explaining how Juliet's character changes over the course of the play. Remember to include evidence from each act of the play to demonstrate how her character changes and develops.

# Mercutio

Mercutio is Romeo's close friend and a kinsman to the Prince. For much of the play, he stands outside the plot, providing a comic counterpoint to Romeo's romantic posturing. However, his death in Act 3, Scene 1 is a turning point in the play and the catalyst for Romeo's downfall.

Mercutio feels that Romeo is acting in a cowardly way by refusing to fight Tybalt – 'O calm, dishonourable, vile submission!' *(Act 3, Scene 1)* – and he is fatally wounded when Romeo tries to stop the fight. As he is dying, he continues to make puns, while also cursing both the Montague and Capulet households.

**Key quotations**

Ask for me tomorrow, and you shall find me a grave man.
*(Mercutio, Act 3, Scene 1)*

A plague a'both your houses!
*(Mercutio, Act 3, Scene 1)*

With his **bawdy vitality** and passionate speeches, Mercutio is considered one of Shakespeare's most memorable characters. His role is a popular one for young actors as it provides a **tour de force** of stage-fighting, punning and horseplay, followed by a dramatic death.

**bawdy** coarse, rude, lewd

**vitality** vigour and energy

**tour de force** a performance requiring great skill that attracts admiration from the audience

In Act 2, Scene 4, Romeo tells the Nurse that Mercutio is someone who **'loves to hear himself talk, and will speak more in a minute than he will stand to in a month'**, which is a way of saying that he is all talk and no action. Explore Mercutio's role in the play and decide if you agree with Romeo's statement.

## Tips for assessment

In your assessment, you need to be specific when referring to characters. Make sure that you know the differences between Benvolio, Mercutio and Tybalt and can write confidently about how each character is presented.

## Nurse

Like Mercutio, the language used by the Nurse often contains **innuendo**, leading some to consider her character to be his female comic counterpart. She is the product of a recognizable Elizabethan world with her prattle about Juliet's childhood, aching bones and gossip. In an age when infant mortality was great, we learn that the Nurse has lost her own daughter and that she is particularly fond of Juliet.

**Key quotations**

Thou wast the prettiest babe that e'er I nurs'd.
*(Nurse, Act 1, Scene 3)*

The Nurse is Juliet's **confidante** and serves as her messenger in arranging her marriage to Romeo. However, after Romeo's banishment, she advises Juliet in Act 3, Scene 5, **'I think it best you married with the County'** (Paris). This sinful suggestion offends Juliet, leading her to end their friendship and from this point onwards Juliet acts alone without the Nurse's assistance.

**confidante** someone to whom secrets are confided
**innuendo** a hint or hidden reference to something rude, often sexual

**Key quotations**

Ancient damnation! O most wicked fiend!
*(Juliet, Act 3, Scene 5)*

**Activity 6**

Re-read the dialogue between Juliet and the Nurse in Act 3, Scene 5 beginning, 'O God! – O Nurse, how shall this be prevented?' to the Nurse's line, 'Marry, I will, and this is wisely done.'

1. In your own words summarize the Nurse's advice to Juliet.

2. Discuss what this dialogue reveals about the Nurse's character and attitudes.

3. Explain how the Nurse's advice changes her relationship with Juliet.

4. Write a speech from the point of view of the Nurse explaining why she has given this advice to Juliet.

# Friar Lawrence

Friar Lawrence's part is the third longest in the play and his importance in the story emphasizes the Italian Catholic setting. He is introduced in the play entering alone with a basket used for gathering herbs, which establishes his connection with the balance of nature. He has been described as a **deus ex machina**, as he is responsible for solving many of the plot dilemmas, such as the hasty marriage of Romeo and Juliet, Romeo's escape to Mantua and, most tellingly, Juliet's false suicide.

> **deus ex machina** a dramatic term for an unlikely solution to a plot dilemma by the sudden introduction of a new character, event or object such as the Friar's sleeping potion

Friar Lawrence is a confidante to Romeo, to whom he advises moderation and patience, and Juliet, for whom he tries to arrange a release from her marriage to Paris. Although he gives the characters hope, his actions do not avert the tragedy and, it could be argued, contribute to it. Although he is acting with the best intentions and hopes to unite the two warring families, his many interventions ultimately lead to the deaths of the young lovers.

**Key quotations**

For this alliance may so happy prove
To turn your households' rancour to pure love.
*(Friar Lawrence, Act 2, Scene 3)*

These violent delights have violent ends
*(Friar Lawrence, Act 2, Scene 6)*

**Tips for assessment**

When writing about characters, remember that they are not real people but characters who have been constructed by a playwright to fulfil certain dramatic functions, and can be interpreted differently by actors, directors and audiences. Remember to use phrases like, 'Shakespeare presents Romeo as...'; 'In this production, the director suggests that Friar Lawrence is...'; or 'There have been many contrasting interpretations of Lady Capulet's character, for instance...'.

**Activity 7**

Friar Lawrence is Romeo's close confidante, as is the Nurse to Juliet. Compare the advice each one gives about:

- love
- getting married
- Romeo's banishment
- Juliet's proposed marriage to Paris.

Discuss which of the two characters is a better advisor and why.

Does the Nurse or Friar Lawrence give Romeo and Juliet the best advice?

## Prince Escales

Prince Escales is the authority figure in *Romeo and Juliet* and, on the three occasions when he appears in the play, is involved in resolving disputes, hearing testimony and issuing judgements. In Act 1, Scene 1, he demands that the 'civil brawls' between the Montagues and Capulets be stopped. In Act 3, Scene 1, he softens his judgement against Romeo from execution to banishment, but maintains the threat of Romeo's death if he does not leave Verona immediately. Finally, in Act 5, Scene 3, he brings about the reconciliation between the Montagues and Capulets. In this **hierarchical** and **patriarchal** society, Prince Escales's voice is the most powerful, ensuring that the other characters obey his wishes, and he is given the final words in the play.

> **hierarchy** a system in which there is a clear ranking of groups or individuals, some having more power and status than others
>
> **patriarchy** a community or society in which men are dominant and hold the power

### Key quotations

If ever you disturb our streets again,
Your lives shall pay the forfeit of the peace.
*(Prince Escales, Act 1, Scene 1)*

For never was a story of more woe
Than this of Juliet and her Romeo.
*(Prince Escales, Act 5, Scene 3)*

### Activity 8

Draw a pyramid showing who has power in Verona with Prince Escales at the top. Place the other characters from the play on the pyramid with the most powerful towards the top and those with the least power and status at the bottom. Discuss the choices you have made and the reasons for these.

## Tybalt

'Fiery' Tybalt, Juliet's cousin, makes a dramatic impact from his first entrance when he joins in the servants' brawl, escalating the action by attacking Benvolio verbally and physically. Although he has relatively few lines (only four more than Romeo's manservant Balthasar), he is a vivid, exciting character, usually at the centre of a conflict. He is described by Mercutio as 'Good King of Cats' *(Act 3, Scene 1)*, suggesting that he possesses a feline, predatory quality as well as being someone who lives dangerously and so needs the 'nine lives' associated with cats. He is a source of danger when he recognizes Romeo at the masked ball and later when he challenges Romeo to a duel. Tybalt's slaying of Mercutio and Romeo's subsequent murder of Tybalt are the tragic turning points in the play.

> **Key quotations**
>
> What, drawn and talk of peace? I hate the word,
> As I hate hell, all Montagues, and thee.
> *(Tybalt, Act 1, Scene 1)*
>
> Boy, this shall not excuse the injuries
> That thou hast done me, therefore turn and draw.
> *(Tybalt, Act 3, Scene 1)*

> **Activity 9**
>
> The following characters die in the play: Mercutio, Tybalt, Paris, Romeo, Juliet and Lady Montague. Create a chart explaining:
>
> - how each character dies
> - if this occurs off or on stage
> - what their dying words were (if known)
> - the importance of his or her death for the plot of the play.

## Lord Capulet

Lord Capulet is the head of an important Veronese family which is feuding with the Montagues. Some find him a somewhat contradictory character. When he is first seen, in Act 1, Scene 1, he has been alerted to the fighting young men and calls out for his sword as if he will join in the fight. His wife, Lady Capulet, reminds him of his age by suggesting he needs a crutch more than a weapon.

Despite his heated first scene, in Act 1, Scene 2, he seems a fond and caring father, describing Juliet as the 'hopeful lady of my earth' and asking that Paris woo her gently, allowing her time to grow up. In Act 1, Scene 5, he also firmly quells Tybalt's attempts to fight at the party when he discovers Romeo is present. However, in Act 3, Scene 5, his extreme anger at Juliet's refusal to marry Paris shows a more irrational and violent side to his character. In the end, he is reconciled with the Montagues.

> **Key quotations**
>
> Hang thee, young baggage, disobedient wretch!
> I tell thee what: get thee to church a'Thursday,
> Or never after look me in the face.
> *(Capulet, Act 3, Scene 5)*

**Activity 10**

Discuss the dramatic implications of Lord Capulet's reactions to Juliet's refusal to marry Paris in Act 3, Scene 5.

# Lady Capulet

Lady Capulet is an intriguing character and can be interpreted in many ways. She has a somewhat distant relationship with Juliet. In Act 1, Scene 3, she at first asks the Nurse to leave so that she can speak privately to Juliet about Paris, saying 'We must talk in secret', but quickly changes her mind, requesting 'Nurse, come back again' as she appears to need the Nurse's support and understanding of Juliet in order to conduct such an important conversation. Lady Capulet tells Juliet that she herself was married and a mother by the time she was Juliet's age, disregarding her husband's caution about the prospect of Juliet marrying at such a young age.

When Juliet refuses to marry Paris in Act 3, Scene 5, Lady Capulet does not protect her daughter from her husband's rage. She leaves the distraught Juliet, saying that she will no longer speak to her.

In this scene from Zeffirelli's 1968 film starring Olivia Hussey, Juliet appears to have a much closer relationship with the Nurse than with Lady Capulet

---

**Key quotations**

Read o'er the volume of young Paris' face,
And find delight writ there with beauty's pen
(*Lady Capulet, Act 1, Scene 3*)

Talk not to me, for I'll not speak a word.
Do as thou wilt, for I have done with thee.
(*Lady Capulet, Act 3, Scene 5*)

---

Some productions suggest that Lady Capulet is much younger than Lord Capulet and that she is unusually fond of the younger male characters, like Tybalt, and this may be why she pleads for Romeo's death for killing Tybalt. Others emphasize her interest in money and status, which explains her eagerness for Juliet to marry.

### Activity 11

Make prompt cards for each of the main characters in the play. Each prompt card should include:

- key quotations
- notes on their importance to the plot
- possible questions you could be asked about that character.

Use these cards as a revision aid.

## Lord and Lady Montague

Lord and Lady Montague are less developed characters than the Capulets, but hold the same high status in Verona society and maintain their side of the ancient feud. At the beginning of the play, like Capulet, Montague is willing to enter into a fight while his wife tries to dissuade him. However, in other instances, they seem more moderate and gentle than the dramatic Capulets. In Act 1, Scene 1, both Montagues express parental affection and concern for Romeo and ask Benvolio to discover why their son is so unhappy.

> **Key quotations**
>
> O where is Romeo? saw you him today?
> Right glad I am he was not at this fray.
> (Lady Montague, Act 1, Scene 1)
>
> Could we but learn from whence his sorrows grow,
> We would as willingly give cure as know.
> (Montague, Act 1, Scene 1)

After Romeo kills Tybalt, in Act 3, Scene 1, Montague pleads with the Prince for his son's life. Unlike the Capulets, in Act 5, Scene 3, Montague enters the tomb alone, as his wife has died due to 'Grief of my son's exile'. Although it occurs offstage, hers is the last death revealed to the audience in the play.

## Activity 12

Write a paragraph contrasting the relationships Romeo and Juliet have with their parents. Consider:

- the freedoms they are given or restrictions placed upon them
- the differences between mother and father
- their reactions to moments of crisis.

# Benvolio

Benvolio is Montague's nephew and Romeo's friend. He teases Romeo about his self-dramatizing infatuation with Rosaline and he and Mercutio persuade him to gatecrash the Capulet party. In Act 3, Scene 1, he tries to persuade Mercutio to go inside to avoid a fight and is obviously aware of the punishment that awaits them should they be caught brawling in public again. After the murder of Mercutio and Tybalt, it is Benvolio who has to explain the events to the Prince.

## Activity 13

Both Mercutio and Benvolio are Romeo's friends, but they seem to serve different functions in the play. Discuss whether you think Mercutio or Benvolio is a better friend to Romeo. Remember to support your ideas with evidence from the text.

# Minor characters

## Paris

This nobleman, also known as the Count or County Paris, wishes to marry Juliet. Lord Capulet finds him a very desirable son-in-law and he is described as being handsome and wealthy by Lady Capulet when she tells Juliet, 'So shall you share all that he doth possess,/ By having him, making yourself no less.' *(Act 1, Scene 3)*. Paris grieves after Juliet's death and is slain by Romeo, who does not at first recognize him. Paris's last wish is to be placed in the Capulet tomb next to Juliet.

Juliet meets Paris when she goes to see Friar Lawrence. Are Paris's unrequited love and death also a tragedy?

> **Key quotations**
>
> Juliet, on Thursday early will I rouse ye;
> Till then adieu, and keep this holy kiss.
> *(Paris, Act 4, Scene 1)*
>
> The obsequies that I for thee will keep
> Nightly shall be to strew thy grave and weep.
> *(Paris, Act 5, Scene 3)*

> **Activity 14**
>
> Once Juliet meets Romeo she no longer considers Paris as a potential husband. However, it could be said that he would be a very appropriate and desirable husband for her and that he truly loves her. Prepare a speech for a debate arguing for or against the statement: 'Paris is the true romantic victim of the play.'

## Apothecary

The apothecary, who appears in Act 5, Scene 1, is a very poor man who attempts to earn a living selling potions and medicines. Romeo knows that the man is starving so convinces him to sell him a 'dram of poison' for the 'life-weary'. The man is reluctant to sell it as he knows it is against the law, but eventually gives Romeo a potion which would 'dispatch' the strongest of men.

> **Key quotations**
>
> My poverty, but not my will, consents.
> *(Apothecary, Act 5, Scene 1)*

**Activity 15**

Both the Apothecary and Friar Lawrence make potions. Compare the portrayal of these two characters.

# Abram and Balthasar

Abram and Balthasar are both servants of the Montagues. Abram takes a major role in the fight in Act 1, Scene 1. Balthasar is Romeo's servant and brings him the news of Juliet's apparent death. He also accompanies Romeo to Juliet's tomb and hides there, so he is able to report to the Prince on the events leading up to the deaths.

# Peter, Sampson and Gregory

Peter, Sampson and Gregory are servants of the Capulet household. Sampson and Gregory form a comic double-act at the play's beginning as they make ribald jokes and try to decide how far they can provoke the Montagues. Peter is the Nurse's personal servant. In Shakespeare's time, Peter was played by Will Kemp, a famous Elizabethan comic actor, so the role was probably enlarged through improvisation to utilize his comic and dancing skills.

**Activity 16**

Choose three adjectives from the list below to describe one of the characters in *Romeo and Juliet*. Tell your partner the three adjectives and see if they can guess who you are describing. Write a paragraph justifying the adjectives you have used to describe your chosen character with evidence from the text.

**wise considerate impulsive temperamental aggressive restless ribald**

**daring violent sensible responsible rash mature comic attractive bawdy**

**innocent fiery shy sensitive romantic loyal verbose secretive mercurial**

**peaceful intelligent gentle beautiful unrealistic proud respectful greedy**

**rude powerful strong determined silly talkative wealthy**

# Writing about characters

*Upgrade*

In your assessment, you will need to demonstrate insight into the characters in the play. This may involve understanding why they speak or act in a certain way, their relationships with other characters or their importance to the plot. Remember that you are not writing about real people but characters who are presented by Shakespeare in a particular way. Since this is a play, these characters will be interpreted differently by actors, directors and designers in various productions. You should consider:

- if the character is sympathetically or critically presented
- how different characters could be interpreted and portrayed by actors
- how the character is introduced to the audience
- what other characters say about the character
- how (and if) the character changes or develops in the course of the play.
- the characters' relationships (e.g. with family, friends or employers)
- any characters with whom this character could be contrasted (e.g. Mercutio and the Nurse or the Apothecary and Friar Lawrence).

# Character map

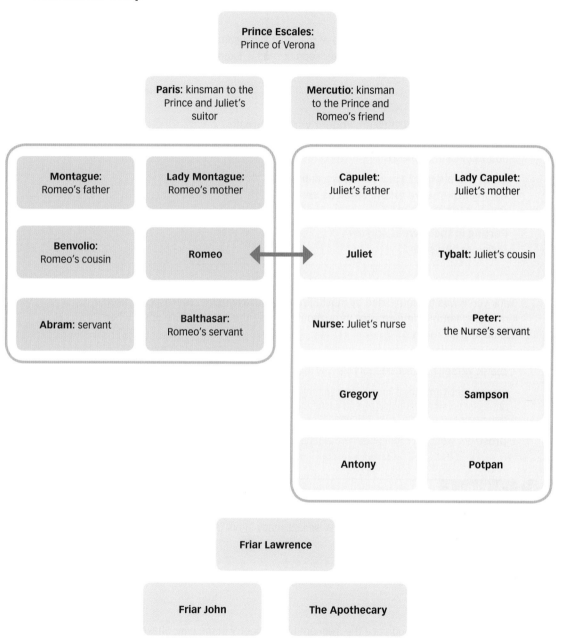

# The language of love

The poetry of *Romeo and Juliet* is one of the most significant aspects of the play, familiar even to people who have never seen or read it. Examples include the following lines from Act 2, Scene 2.

> **Key quotations**
>
> But soft, what light through yonder window breaks?
> It is the east, and Juliet is the sun.
> *(Romeo, Act 2, Scene 2)*
>
> What's in a name? That which we call a rose
> By any other word would smell as sweet
> *(Juliet, Act 2, Scene 2)*
>
> Parting is such sweet sorrow
> *(Juliet, Act 2, Scene 2)*

The play is mainly written in **blank verse** with only 10 per cent of its lines in **prose**. Blank verse was the form used by most Elizabethan playwrights. Shakespeare used a form called **iambic pentameter** throughout the play, though there are times when this pattern is broken.

**blank verse** unrhymed lines of poetry with a regular metre

**iambic pentameter** a line of verse with ten syllables, forming five 'feet', where the stress falls on the second syllable in each foot, e.g. 'di dum' as in 'He jests at scars that never felt a wound.' *(Act 2, Scene 2)*

**prose** any writing in continuous form without rhythm or rhyme

**Activity 1**

Re-read Act 3, Scene 1 and note when the characters are speaking in verse and when in prose. Mercutio, in particular, speaks many of his lines in prose. Discuss what this says about him as a character and how it affects the rhythm of the scene.

# Sonnets

As if signalling to the audience the frequent use of poetry in the play, Shakespeare begins it with a sonnet. The Chorus's 14-line speech introduces many of the **themes** in the play, such as fate, love and violence, and foreshadows the deaths of the lovers. It ends with a stately **rhyming couplet**, encouraging the audience to listen carefully to the play: 'The which if you with patient ears attend,/ What here shall miss, our toil shall strive to mend.' (Chorus, The Prologue) This solemn mood is then swiftly challenged by the irreverent entrance of the Capulet servants at the outset of Act 1 Scene 1, who are speaking prose and making boisterous jokes.

> **rhyming couplet** two consecutive lines which rhyme
>
> **theme** a subject or idea that is repeated or developed in a literary work

Act 1, Scene 5 has the most remarkable use of sonnets. When Romeo first speaks to Juliet, they share a sonnet which ends with a kiss on the rhyming couplet 'sake/take'. They begin another sonnet which is then interrupted by the Nurse. The ease with which the two lovers share the rhythm, form and imagery of the sonnet is symbolic of their mutual passion and empathy.

The Chorus delivers his final sonnet to draw Act 1 to a close, which, in contrast to the Romeo and Juliet love sonnets, emphasizes the danger into which the young lovers are entering.

## Activity 2

Re-read the shared sonnet between Romeo and Juliet in Act 1, Scene 5, beginning with Romeo's line, **'If I profane with my unworthiest hand'**, and ending with Romeo's line, **'Then from my lips, by thine, my sin is purg'd.'**

1. Write out this sonnet as if it was spoken by only one person. Note the rhyme scheme, the stressed and unstressed syllables, and the final rhyming couplet.

2. Highlight in different colours the lines spoken by each character.

3. What similarities and differences can you discover between the two characters from what they say in the sonnet?

# Rhyming couplets

Although most of the play is written in blank verse, Shakespeare also uses **rhyming couplets**. These are usually in sections of high romance or as a concluding couplet at the end of a sonnet, scene or act to bring a sense of completion.

> **Key quotations**
>
> Did my heart love till now? foreswear it, sight!
> For I ne'er saw true beauty till this night.
> (Romeo, Act 1, Scene 5)

**Activity 3**

Many scholars feel that Romeo's use of language grows and changes throughout the play. Some feel that his love poetry is more clichéd and predictable when speaking of Rosaline than when he sees and falls in love with Juliet.

1. Compare Romeo's use of rhyming couplets to describe his feelings for Rosaline in his speech in Act 1, Scene 1, beginning with the line, **'Well, in that hit you miss: she'll not be hit'** with his reaction to seeing Juliet for the first time in Act 1, Scene 5, beginning, **'O she doth teach the torches to burn bright!'**

2. Explain why you think Shakespeare wrote both of these passages in rhyming couplets. What similarities and differences can you note?

3. For a more dramatic contrast, compare Romeo's use of rhyming couplets with those used by the mechanicals in Act 5 of *A Midsummer Night's Dream* (see Thisbe's speech on page 31 of the Context section of this book).

# Imagery

*Romeo and Juliet* is rich with imagery, often dealing with oppositions such as light and dark or love and hate. One way of emphasizing conflicting emotions is the use of **oxymorons**, which Romeo utilizes in Act 1, Scene 1:

> **Key quotations**
>
> Why then, O brawling love, O loving hate,
> O any thing of nothing first create!
> O heavy lightness, serious vanity,
> Misshapen chaos of well-seeming forms,
> Feather of lead, bright smoke, cold fire, sick health,
> Still-waking sleep, that is not what it is!
> *(Romeo, Act 1, Scene 1)*

**Activity 4**

1. Read the key quotation above and write a paragraph explaining what the oxymorons suggest about Romeo's emotional state.

2. Try creating your own original oxymorons. Share your work with a partner and discuss the effect you have achieved.

There are many examples of **personification** in *Romeo and Juliet*. Playwrights can use personification as a way of making vivid and clear ideas which might be difficult for an audience to imagine otherwise.

## Activity 5

Look at the quotations below and decide what is being personified and what human qualities are suggested by it. The first one has been done for you.

1.  **Alas that Love, so gentle in his view,**
    **Should be so tyrannous and rough in proof!**
    *(Benvolio, Act 1, Scene 1)*

    Personified: Love
    Qualities: At first it seems gentle, but in experience is cruel and controlling.

2.  **Now old desire doth in his death-bed lie,**
    **And young affection gapes to be his heir**
    *(Chorus, Act 1, Scene 5)*

3.  **O Fortune, Fortune, all men call thee fickle**
    *(Juliet, Act 3, Scene 5)*

4.  **Death is my son-in-law, Death is my heir**
    *(Capulet, Act 4, Scene 5)*

Shakespeare also uses many **metaphors** throughout *Romeo and Juliet*. For example, the Nurse says of Paris 'he's a flower' (Act 1, Scene 3), echoing Lady Capulet's metaphor chosen to express Paris's handsome appearance. Romeo uses numerous metaphors in Act 1, Scene 1 to express his thoughts about love.

> **metaphor** a figure of speech applied to something to suggest a resemblance, without using the words 'like' or 'as'
>
> **oxymoron** a figure of speech in which two contradictory or extremely unlikely ideas or images are joined
>
> **personification** when human qualities are given to something non-human, such as an object or an idea

> **Key quotations**
>
> **Love is a smoke made with the fume of sighs,**
> **Being purg'd, a fire sparkling in lovers' eyes,**
> **Being vex'd, a sea nourish'd with loving tears.**
> **What is it else? a madness most discreet,**
> **A choking gall, and a preserving sweet.**
> *(Romeo, Act 1, Scene 1)*

## Activity 6

Read Lady Capulet's description of Paris in Act 1, Scene 3, beginning with the line, 'What say you, can you love the gentleman?' to 'By having him, making yourself no less.' Decide what **extended metaphor** she uses here and how it helps to explain how she feels about Paris.

**extended metaphor** a metaphor which is developed for several lines or more

The play also includes imagery on the following topics:

- nature (e.g. in Friar Lawrence's opening speech in Act 2, Scene 3 and in Romeo and Juliet's parting in Act 3, Scene 5)
- light and darkness (e.g. when Romeo first sees Juliet in Act 1, Scene 5 and in the balcony scene in Act 2, Scene 2)
- religion (e.g. in Romeo and Juliet's shared sonnet in Act 1, Scene 5)
- time (in Juliet's opening speeches in Act 2, Scene 5 and Act 3, Scene 2)
- dreams (e.g. in Mercutio's Queen Mab speech in Act 1, Scene 4 and Romeo's opening speech in Act 5, Scene 1).

In addition, throughout the play, marriage and love are united with death as in Act 1, Scene 5 when Juliet declares 'My grave is like to be my wedding bed.'

Juliet lies on her 'death' bed here in the 1996 film *William Shakespeare's Romeo + Juliet*, perhaps looking like a young bride

## Tips for assessment

*Upgrade*

In your assessment, you will need to be precise in your use of literary terms. Compile a personal glossary of literary terms and find several examples for each technique.

## Activity 7

Choose one of the imagery topics listed above. Make a diagram identifying quotations in which such imagery is used and giving your analysis of the examples. The example below has been started for you.

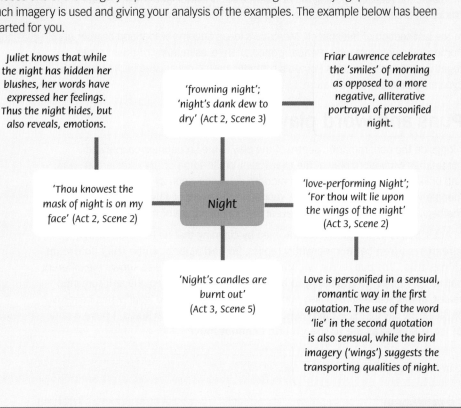

Juliet knows that while the night has hidden her blushes, her words have expressed her feelings. Thus the night hides, but also reveals, emotions.

'frowning night'; 'night's dank dew to dry' (Act 2, Scene 3)

Friar Lawrence celebrates the 'smiles' of morning as opposed to a more negative, alliterative portrayal of personified night.

'Thou knowest the mask of night is on my face' (Act 2, Scene 2)

**Night**

'love-performing Night'; 'For thou wilt lie upon the wings of the night' (Act 3, Scene 2)

'Night's candles are burnt out' (Act 3, Scene 5)

Love is personified in a sensual, romantic way in the first quotation. The use of the word 'lie' in the second quotation is also sensual, while the bird imagery ('wings') suggests the transporting qualities of night.

## Queen Mab speech

Many students consider Mercutio's 'Queen Mab' speech in Act 1, Scene 4 challenging, finding themselves in agreement with Romeo's assessment **'Thou talk'st of nothing.'** Before the speech, Romeo is trying to find excuses to avoid going to the Capulet party and announces that he has had a dream, the implication being that it has made him feel that something bad is going to happen. Mercutio claims that he too had a dream, **'That dreamers often lie'**, and goes on to describe Queen Mab, a tiny fairy who is responsible for sleepers' dreams.

In the first section of the speech, Mercutio uses a number of images to establish how small Queen Mab is and how she travels in her **'chariot'** which is **'an empty hazel-nut'**.

In the second section of the speech, he recounts all the different sleepers that she visits and what their dreams are. Perhaps unsurprisingly, lovers dream of love and soldiers of war. More tellingly, lawyers are dreaming of 'fees' rather than justice and parsons are dreaming of a 'tithe-pig' (a form of payment) rather than religion. Mercutio, the realist, is poking fun at Romeo, the dreamer, and the importance he places on dreams, which Mercutio believes are 'the children of an idle brain'.

In the last section of the speech, Mercutio's ideas become wilder and coarser until Romeo interrupts him with 'Peace, peace...' Here, as in many of their scenes together, the audience sees Romeo's romantic nature contrasted with Mercutio's cynical opinion of human nature.

# Puns and word play

Alongside the rich, romantic poetry of the play is the sometimes coarse and sometimes witty word play of the characters. While some of the jokes are **archaic** and unlikely to raise a smile from a modern audience (such as the pun on 'colliers' (people who carry coal) and 'choler' (anger) in the exchange between the servants at the beginning of the play), others reveal the playful nature of the characters.

In Act 1, Scene 4, Mercutio teases Romeo by claiming that he has dreamt that 'dreamers often lie'. Romeo wittily replies, 'In bed asleep, while they do dream things true.' The pun on the two meanings of the word 'lie' also shows the different natures of Romeo, who is happy to be a dreamer, and Mercutio, the anti-romantic realist. In this scene Romeo also puns on the words 'sole' and 'soul' when he refuses to dance, by saying, 'You have dancing shoes/ With nimble soles, I have a soul of lead/ So stakes me to the ground I cannot move.'

> **archaic** very old and no longer in use

## Activity 8

Read Mercutio's lines after he has been wounded in Act 3, Scene 1, beginning, **'No, 'tis not so deep as a well...'** to **'And soundly too. Your houses!'** In this dramatic section, Mercutio alternates jokes and puns with pleas for help and curses.

1. Break down Mercutio's lines and identify when he is making a joke and when he is being serious.

2. Imagine that you are a director and explain how you would have an actor play this scene.

# Writing about language

*Upgrade*

When writing about *Romeo and Juliet,* it is vital that you demonstrate that you understand the language in the play. Even if your question does not seem to be asking you directly about language, you will be expected to demonstrate how Shakespeare uses various literary techniques and language choices in order to convey his ideas.

In order to prepare for this, practise doing the following:

- Write about the play *as a play*, not as a novel or story.

- Show an awareness of the playwright by using phrases like 'Shakespeare presents...' or 'Shakespeare contrasts...'.

- Pick out short key quotations to support your ideas.

- Use literary terminology correctly, but don't just spot the technique – explain the effect created.

- Be aware when there are several possible interpretations of a line.

- Highlight contrasts and shifts in mood or tone.

- When writing about verse, note when there are changes in the metre or when lines are shared or interrupted, explaining what this tells us about the characters.

- Explore the differences between the various characters' dialogue, for example, how Mercutio's lines differ from those of Romeo or the Nurse.

- Analyse patterns in language and reoccurring motifs and images such as those for night, fate, religion or nature.

# Themes

The many exciting **themes** explored in *Romeo and Juliet* are, in part, responsible for its lasting appeal. Every generation has an interest in themes such as love, violence, youth versus age, and rebellion against society. As you read the play, note when a particular theme is highlighted; when you see it performed, note how the production emphasizes one or more themes more than others.

The love story of Romeo and Juliet has inspired a wide range of art forms including paintings, ballet, opera – and mass-produced postcards like this one

## Love

Love is the most obvious theme in the play and the very names Romeo and Juliet are now used to conjure images of passionate lovers. Besides the mutual romantic love between Romeo and Juliet, there are other examples of love to be explored such as **unrequited love** and parental love.

> **unrequited love** unreturned love, where the person who is in love is not loved in return by the object of their affection

### Unrequited love

At the beginning of the play, Romeo is suffering from unrequited love for Rosaline. This love is painful for him and leads him to abandon his friends and family, and to seek solitude. He uses metaphors to describe the pain of his condition.

> **Key quotations**
>
> What is it else? a madness most discreet,
> A choking gall, and a preserving sweet.
> *(Romeo, Act 1, Scene 1)*

However, Romeo's friends do not seem to take his 'love' seriously, teasing him about it and encouraging him to go out and 'Examine other beauties' *(Act 1, Scene 1)*.

Romeo is not the only character in the play who suffers unrequited love, as Paris thinks he is in love with Juliet, but she does not return it. His reaction to Juliet's apparent death in Act 4, Scene 5 appears heartfelt and in Act 5 he dies, protecting her tomb from what he believes will be desecration by a rival family. His dying words are a request to be buried with Juliet.

> **Key quotations**
>
> O love! O life! not life, but love in death!
> *(Paris, Act 4, Scene 5)*
>
> The obsequies that I for thee will keep
> Nightly shall be to strew thy grave and weep.
> *(Paris, Act 5, Scene 3)*
>
> Open the tomb, lay me with Juliet.
> *(Paris, Act 5, Scene 3)*

## Love at first sight

When Romeo and Juliet meet they fall in love at first sight. Some use the French term **coup de foudre** to describe the lightning-fast way in which they fall in love. Romeo's very first words to Juliet, in the form of a sonnet, are a request for a kiss. In their first meeting, Shakespeare interweaves religious imagery ('holy shrine', 'pilgrim', 'saints') with Romeo's playful physical pursuit of Juliet.

> **coup de foudre** an amazing or unusually quick and dramatic occurrence; from the French meaning 'a lightning flash'

Cupid, the Roman god of attraction and desire, is mentioned many times in the play. When shot with one of Cupid's arrows, one is meant to be filled with uncontrollable desire. Romeo's friends, particularly Mercutio, take a much more irreverent attitude to love, with Cupid's arrows being mocked as **'the blind bow-boy's butt-shaft'** *(Act 2, Scene 4)*. He ridicules Romeo's romantic nature, taking a more ribald and harsh view.

> **Key quotations**
>
> If love be rough with you, be rough with love
> *(Mercutio, Act 1, Scene 4)*
>
> Romeo! humours! madman! passion! lover!
> *(Mercutio, Act 2, Scene 1)*

 **Activity 1**

Find all the different times Cupid is mentioned in *Romeo and Juliet* and discuss his particular relevance to the play.

# Parental love

Parental love is evident in the Montagues' concern for Romeo in Act 1, Scene 1 and later in his mother's despair and death in reaction to his banishment. The Capulets present a more complex picture of parental love. In Act 1, Scene 2, Lord Capulet seems genuinely concerned about his daughter's well-being and happiness. He says he will not dictate who she marries, so that Paris must woo her and win her heart.

> **Key quotations**
>
> But woo her, gentle Paris, get her heart,
> My will to her consent is but a part;
> And she agreed, within her scope of choice
> Lies my consent and fair according voice.
> *(Capulet, Act 1, Scene 2)*

The speech above suggests that Capulet hopes that Juliet will have a happy marriage based on love. However, his wife, although still asking if Juliet can 'love the gentleman' *(Act 1, Scene 3)*, seems to be more actively encouraging a hasty arranged marriage. This may be because her relationship with her daughter is more distant. Instead the Nurse seems to fulfil a more loving role and it is to her that Juliet turns to assist with her secret marriage. However, the Nurse can also seem opportunistic; for example, when she describes Juliet to Romeo, she ends by mentioning that whoever marries her 'Shall have the chinks' *(Act 1, Scene 5)*, meaning he will receive plenty of money. She is also quick to suggest that Juliet abandon Romeo and marry Paris when Lord Capulet commands it.

**Activity 2**

What clues can you find in the play about the state of the marriages of the Montagues and Capulets? Discuss what these suggest about the relationships between Lord and Lady Capulet, and Lord and Lady Montague.

# Doomed love

Suggestions of doomed love are present throughout the play. The first mention of love is in the Prologue: 'a pair of star-cross'd lovers take their life'. Throughout the play there are words of unease expressed about the lovers' relationship, even during the romantic balcony scene. Meanwhile Friar Lawrence also issues warnings about their love.

Love and death are joined in Act 5. When Romeo drinks his potion in Scene 3, he toasts 'Here's to my love!'. When Juliet awakes, she attempts to kiss poison from Romeo's lips. She then takes his dagger and stabs herself, ensuring that she dies with him. Death and love are joined not only in the words of the characters but also in their actions.

However, the end of the play can also be viewed as a triumph of love. Romeo and Juliet's love has not only brought their two families together, but they are joined forever in death.

# Hate and violence

The opening Prologue announces that the play will be about hate and violence, as well as love. Words like 'grudge', 'mutiny' and 'rage' prepare the audience for the first fight, which happens only minutes into the play. Shakespeare never specifies the source of the 'ancient grudge' but many productions seek to find a logical obstacle to the love of the young lovers, such as rival ethnic gangs and turf war in *West Side Story*.

Whatever the cause of the feud between the families, it is a key plot point and leads to the tragedy. In Act 1, Scene 1, the feud is shown to affect every member of both

The rival gangs in the 50th anniversary world tour of *West Side Story* stand up to each other

households, from the lowliest servants to the most elderly family members. Tybalt is the most violent character in the play, threatening Benvolio with death in his very first line. His declaration that he hates peace suggests that his desire to fight goes beyond the cause of the feud and is more an aspect of his own violent and angry personality. On his second appearance, he demands a rapier in order to kill Romeo at the masked ball. Even Capulet, who can be hot-headed himself, seems to find Tybalt's tendency towards violence wrong and sternly criticizes his behaviour and presumption at the masked ball.

The fights in the play often begin because a character believes he has been shamed and that the honour of the family needs to be protected. Abram reacts to the insulting gesture of the biting of the thumb. Tybalt believes the family ceremony has been shamed by the appearance of the Montagues and then follows this with a direct challenge to Romeo for his insolence. Mercutio fights Tybalt, ashamed of Romeo's apparently embarrassing and cowardly 'submission'. Paris challenges Romeo as he believes that Romeo plans to insult the Capulets by defacing Juliet's tomb.

**Activity 3**

Copy and complete the chart below, analysing the key fights in the play.

| Act and scene | Who is fighting | Cause of fight | Important lines |
|---|---|---|---|
| Act 1, Scene 1 | First the servants of the Montague and Capulet households, later joined by higher members of the households, including Benvolio (who tries to keep the peace), Tybalt and Lords Montague and Capulet | Sampson, a Capulet servant, makes an insulting gesture to two Montague servants, Abram and Balthasar | 'Do you bite your thumb at us, sir?' 'As I hate hell, all Montagues, and thee.' |
| Act 3, Scene 1 | Mercutio and Tybalt, and then Romeo and Tybalt | | |
| Act 5, Scene 3 | Romeo and Paris | | |

It is the function of the Prince to try to control the fighting between the families. We learn that the first fight we witness is actually the third of the recent 'civil brawls' (public fights) *(Act 1, Scene 1)* between the families. In his urgency to control the bloodshed on the streets, the Prince issues a strong, commanding speech in which he repeats the word 'peace' three times, reinforcing this as his goal. In the final speech of the play, he refers to a 'glooming peace' *(Act 5, Scene 3)*, suggesting that though they have finally reached a reconciliation, it has been at a very steep and depressing cost.

# Youth, age and time

The youthfulness of the protagonists is mentioned many times in the play. Juliet's age is given very precisely, as we learn that she will be fourteen in just over two weeks. Although an exact age for Romeo is not provided, he is generally thought to be a little older than Juliet. At the beginning of the play, he has more experience of the world, but by the end, she seems the more mature.

Time passes very quickly in the play, with the whole action taking only four days. Four days in the life of an elderly person may seem like nothing, but Romeo and Juliet must have a lifetime of passion, including their single married night together, in those four days. The plot of the play hinges on an ancient feud, which remains very fresh for the Monatagues and Capulets, and there are different attitudes towards time presented by the various characters. In Act 1, Scene 5, Capulet discusses how quickly time has gone since they last attended a masked ball, as he cannot believe it has been as long as 30 years. On the other hand, time can pass very slowly for the young lovers when they are apart, so Juliet urges night to hurry so that they can be together, **'Gallop apace'** *(Act 3, Scene 2)*, or to slow down so they can stay together, **'Yond light is not daylight'** *(Act 3, Scene 5)*.

## Activity 4

Read the quotations below and explain what each one tells us about the character's attitude towards age.

1. **My child is yet a stranger in the world**
   *(Capulet, Act 1, Scene 2)*

2. **Younger than she are happy mothers made.**
   *(Paris, Act 1, Scene 2)*

3. **Well, think of marriage now; younger than you,**
   **Here in Verona, ladies of esteem,**
   **Are made already mothers.**
   *(Lady Capulet, Act 1, Scene 3)*

4. **... Young men's love then lies**
   **Not truly in their hearts, but in their eyes.**
   *(Friar Lawrence, Act 2, Scene 3)*

5. **Now I have stain'd the childhood of our joy**
   *(Romeo, Act 3, Scene 3)*

In key scenes, Romeo's youth and rashness are contrasted with Friar Lawrence's age and wisdom, and Juliet's impatience and innocence with her Nurse's slowness and **ribaldry**. Age is presented as both commanding respect and inviting ridicule.

An important aspect of the tragedy is the youth of the protagonists and the sacrifice of their young lives, which are so full of promise and hope.

> **ribaldry** crude talk or behaviour

# Friendship

A key difference between Romeo and Juliet is that Romeo is frequently seen in the company of his friends, whereas Juliet's sheltered upbringing suggests that her Nurse is her closest confidante.

Benvolio and Mercutio are contrasting friends. Benvolio's first lines, in Act 1, Scene 1, establish him as a peacemaker: 'Part, fools!/ Put up your swords, you know not what you do.' Mercutio claims Benvolio is 'as hot a Jack in thy mood as any in Italy' *(Act 3, Scene 1)*, but Montague seems to trust Benvolio not only to explain the cause of the first brawl, but also to discover the source of Romeo's despair. In his first scene with Romeo, Benvolio gently teases him and attempts to draw him out.

Mercutio, on the other hand, is a mercurial, changeable, energetic character, ready to joke or fight as the occasion demands. Both Benvolio and Mercutio regret the changes in Romeo that love has caused. When Mercutio is killed, it is to avenge his death that Romeo kills Tybalt.

## Activity 5

Read the speech below and discuss what it reveals about Romeo's friendship with Mercutio.

This gentleman, the prince's near ally,
My very friend, hath got his mortal hurt
In my behalf; my reputation stain'd
With Tybalt's slander – Tybalt, that an hour
Hath been my cousin. O sweet Juliet,
Thy beauty hath made me effeminate,
And in my tempter soften'd valour's steel!
*(Romeo, Act 3, Scene 1)*

# Rebellion against society

Romeo and Juliet live in a strict, hierarchal world where their families, their society and their religion place restrictions upon their actions. In Elizabethan times, the expectation was that children should obey their parents, marry someone suitable from an appropriate family, and have the marriage blessed by the Church and celebrated by friends and family. In Act 1, Scene 5, Juliet could refuse to speak to a young man she doesn't know, or Romeo, upon learning that Juliet is the daughter of Lord Capulet, could vow never to see her again and that would be the end of the play. However, both characters ignore danger and pursue their own desires. Other instances when characters break the rules of their society include when:

- Romeo, Benvolio and Mercutio gatecrash the Capulet party
- Tybalt and Mercutio ignore the Prince's ruling that they must no longer 'disturb our streets' (Act 1, Scene 1)
- Juliet refuses to marry the man of her parents' choice
- Friar Lawrence behaves deceptively by conducting a secret wedding and assisting Juliet in faking her death
- Romeo bribes the Apothecary into selling him poison, which is against the law
- Romeo breaks into Juliet's tomb, which would be against the norms of behaviour
- both Romeo and Juliet commit suicide, which is against their religious beliefs.

**Key quotations**

To go with Paris to Saint Peter's Church,
Or I will drag thee on a hurdle thither.
(Capulet, Act 3, Scene 5)

The world is not thy friend, nor the world's law,
The world affords no law to make thee rich
(Romeo, Act 5, Scene 1)

Some productions make explicit criticisms of the society against which Romeo and Juliet are rebelling. For example, in *West Side Story*, the few adults shown are unsympathetic or ineffectual and many of the young gang members come from dysfunctional or alienated families. In Michael Bogdanov's 1986 stage version for the Royal Shakespeare Company (RSC), Romeo and Juliet are placed in a noisy, harsh, materialistic world.

## Activity 6

Imagine you have been asked to direct a production of *Romeo and Juliet*. You must decide on a setting for your production and suggest what the source of the ancient feud might be. Consider the following questions.

- Are you going to update your production and/or set it in a particular country?
- What is the source of conflict between the Capulets and Montagues?
- How will you make clear to the audience the differences between the Montagues and Capulets?

# Fate

It could be argued that Romeo and Juliet have no control over their actions as their love and deaths are determined by fate. The Prologue informs us that they are 'star-cross'd', 'misadventur'd' and 'death-mark'd', all suggesting that they are doomed. This could be supported by their sudden and possibly inexplicable infatuation and the series of coincidences (e.g. Friar Lawrence's letter not being delivered due to a plague in Mantua, Romeo dying only moments before Juliet awakens) that lead to their downfall.

## Activity 7

Read the speech below carefully and then answer the following questions.

1. What does 'hanging in the stars' mean?
2. What metaphor does Romeo use for fate controlling his life?
3. What predictions does he make that come true at the end of play?

I fear too early, for my mind misgives
Some consequence yet hanging in the stars
Shall bitterly begin his fearful date
With this night's revels, and expire the term
Of a despised life clos'd in my breast,
By some vile forfeit of untimely death.
But He that hath the steerage of my course
Direct my sail! On, lusty gentlemen.
*(Romeo, Act 1, Scene 4)*

**Activity 8**

After killing Tybalt, Romeo cries out **'O, I am fortune's fool.'** *(Act 3, Scene 1)*
Working with a partner, experiment with different ways of saying this line. You
could try saying it as if:

- you suddenly realize you have lost everything that is important to you

- you are crying out to the heavens or Lady Fortune in despair

- you are eerily calm and still

- you cannot believe how foolish you have been

- you are explaining to the audience why you have killed Tybalt.

Decide which reading you like best and why.

# Writing about themes

*Upgrade*

In your assessment, you may be asked to write specifically about a
theme like love, violence or fate, or you may discuss the themes presented in a given
extract or scene. When writing about themes, remember to discuss how language and
form are used and provide clear examples.

Try revising some of these possible theme-based questions:

1. To what extent do you agree with the following statement: Love is presented as a
   destructive force in *Romeo and Juliet*?

2. How does Shakespeare present the relationship between parents and children in
   the play?

3. Look closely at the language in Act 2, Scene 2. How is love portrayed in the play?

4. How does Shakespeare use the Prologue to introduce the themes of the play?

5. What is the importance of the role of Prince Escales in establishing the key themes of
   the play?

6. Compare how two different productions depict the cause of the 'ancient feud' in
   *Romeo and Juliet*.

7. How is nature imagery used to emphasize the key themes of the play?

8. How important is the role of fate in *Romeo and Juliet*?

To prepare to answer this type of question, you will need to:

- locate key quotations which illustrate each of the themes

- consider the importance of the theme in different scenes and acts of the play

- find recurring images or motifs associated with that theme (such as Cupid for love).

## The Elizabethan theatre

In Elizabethan times, theatre-going was a popular but controversial activity. Although the actors often had the protection of the Queen and other important figures, they had two great enemies: the plague and the **Puritans**. Theatres were frequently shut down due to fears of the audience spreading infection or because plays were thought to be encouraging disruptive or lewd behaviour.

The plague was a real threat at this time and between 1592 and 1594, 20,000 people, a fifth of London's population, succumbed to it. Some scholars believe that Shakespeare may have begun writing *Romeo and Juliet* during this time when many young people were dying. Shakespeare's own son, Hamnet, died in Stratford-upon-Avon in 1596 at a time when there was an outbreak of the plague in the area.

The first performances of *Romeo and Juliet* are thought to have taken place in 1596–97 at the Curtain Theatre. The only casting of which we can be quite certain is that of the comic actor Will Kemp, who played the role of Peter. It is likely that Richard Burbage, the company's **leading man** at this time, played Romeo. Juliet would have been played by a boy actor, as women were not allowed to appear onstage.

Typically, Elizabethan theatres were circular (the Curtain was described as a 'wooden O' in *Henry V*) with 'thrust' stages, which jutted out into the audience. There was roofing for some of the seated audience and the stage, but 'groundlings' (those who paid the least for their tickets) stood in an area called 'the yard' or 'the pit' in front of the stage which was open to the elements. There was

The modern Globe Theatre is a replica of an Elizabethan theatre, with an enclosed space at the back of the stage and a balcony

no electricity, so performances were during daylight hours and dialogue was often used to make clear the time of day of a given scene. Only essential props or pieces of stage furniture would be used, but the actors would wear costumes, which sometimes consisted of clothing handed down from aristocratic families.

> **leading man** the actor playing the main role, often one of romantic interest
>
> **Puritans** a group of strict English Protestants who were against social pleasures such as the theatre, which they thought were an encouragement to vice

### Activity 1

Closely read Act 2, Scene 2 and note every reference to night in the dialogue. Discuss how these references would help the Elizabethan audience.

# Dramatic devices

Playwrights use dramatic devices to create particular effects for the audience. There are several important dramatic devices used in *Romeo and Juliet*.

## Soliloquy

A soliloquy is where a character voices aloud their innermost thoughts for the audience to hear. These moments usually occur when a character is alone on stage – the word 'soliloquy' derives from the Latin, meaning to speak alone. An actor may deliver a soliloquy as if they are lost in their own thoughts, but they may also speak to the audience directly.

**Activity 2**

Re-read Juliet's soliloquy from Act 2, Scene 5, beginning, **'The clock struck nine when I did send the Nurse'** to **'Unwieldy, slow, heavy, and pale as lead'**.

1. Make notes on the following:
   - What words does Juliet use to highlight her impatience?
   - What private thoughts are being expressed in this soliloquy which Juliet might not say if she was speaking to someone else?
   - How is Juliet different in this scene from when she speaks to her parents?
   - How does this speech make the subsequent dialogue with the Nurse more dramatic and amusing?

2. Find other soliloquies from the play and write a paragraph about the dramatic function of each.

## Monologue

A speech spoken by one character not necessarily alone on stage is called a monologue. For example, Mercutio's 'Queen Mab' speech in Act 1, Scene 4 is a monologue as he is speaking to Romeo and Benvolio.

**Activity 3**

Imagine you are a director who has been asked to stage the 'Queen Mab' speech. What advice would you give to the actor playing Mercutio on how to deliver this monologue? Think about the tone of voice, movements, gestures and facial expressions.

## Dialogue

Dialogue is words spoken between two or more characters. Elizabethan audiences placed great importance on the sound of the speeches in a play and would refer to going to 'hear' a play rather than see it. Notice that in the Prologue, the audience is urged to use their 'patient ears', emphasizing the importance of listening. Some characters in the play have very distinctive ways of speaking. It would be impossible, for example, to mistake the Nurse's dialogue for Lady Capulet's.

### Activity 4

Read the following extract from the play. The characters' names have been removed, but as you read, decide which characters are speaking. Share your ideas and discuss what is distinctive about the way each of the three characters speaks.

**Character 1**  Peace, I have done. God mark thee to his grace,
Thou wast the prettiest babe that e'er I nurs'd.
And I might live to see thee married once,
I have my wish.

**Character 2**  Marry, that 'marry'' is the very theme
I came to talk of. Tell me, daughter Juliet,
How stands your dispositions to be married?

**Character 3**  It is an honour that I dream not of.

**Character 1**  An honour! were not I thine only nurse,
I would say thou hadst suck'd wisdom from thy teat.

**Character 2**  Well, think of marriage now; younger than you,
Here in Verona, ladies of esteem,
Are made already mothers. By my count,
I was your mother much upon these years
That you are now a maid. Thus then in brief:
The valiant Paris seeks you for his love.

**Character 1**  A man, young lady! lady, such a man
As all the world – Why, he's a man of wax.

## Stage directions

Stage directions suggest the actions of the characters on stage, including their entrances, exits and key movements. Shakespeare used relatively few stage directions, especially when compared to some later playwrights. An entire stage fight may be summed up with the stage direction 'They fight.' This gives actors and directors a great deal of freedom to interpret the actions.

## Activity 5

1. Skim-read the play to find any stage directions. Identify any specific details contained in the stage directions which help you to understand the characters and plot.

2. Often the actors' actions are suggested by the dialogue. For example, when Romeo says **'See how she leans her cheek upon her hand!'**, in Act 2, Scene 2, we assume that the actress should be doing this. Pick out any other 'hidden' stage directions you can find in the dialogue.

## Stage fighting

Elizabethan gentlemen would be skilled in swordplay and actors would be expected to handle rapiers, swords and daggers with expertise, making sure that their fighting was both convincing and safe. They would also use animal bladders filled with sheep's blood hidden in their costumes to increase the excitement and gore during some stage fights.

## Activity 6

Re-read Mercutio's speech from Act 2, Scene 4, beginning, **'More than Prince of Cats'** and ending **'Ah, the immortal 'passado', the 'punto reverso', the 'hay'!'** Here, he is describing how Tybalt fences and mentions specific fencing terms.

• What do you learn about Tybalt from this speech?

• If you were a director, how would you stage this speech? Draw a storyboard to highlight the main actions.

---

**hay** a stab to the heart, possibly fatal as it derives from the Italian hai meaning 'you have it'

**passado** a manoeuvre in which a sword is thrust forward and one foot advanced at the same time

**punto reverso** the left-to-right cut of a sword

---

## Staging

Shakespeare's plays move easily from scene to scene, often needing only the slightest of changes such as bringing on a simple prop or a piece of stage furniture to suggest a different setting. In the Elizabethan theatre, most of the action would take place on the rectangular thrust stage, but there was also a trapdoor which would be used for special effects; a curtained 'discovery space' which was a small room towards the back of the stage; and, most importantly for *Romeo and Juliet*, a balcony area where scenes like Act 2, Scene 2 could take place and where the musicians would perform.

# The play in performance

*Romeo and Juliet* was immediately popular during Shakespeare's time and has been reinterpreted and reinvented countless times over the centuries to suit the interests, tastes and concerns of subsequent generations.

In 1750, the acclaimed actor-manager David Garrick produced the play and played Romeo. He raised Juliet's age to 18 and deleted any mention of Rosaline, worried that audiences would feel that Romeo was unforgivably shallow and fickle. He added a scene allowing Romeo to live long enough for the two lovers to have a last romantic parting scene.

## Activity 7

In 1815, the famous actor Edmund Kean played Romeo. Read the following description by a contemporary critic of his performance of the banishment scene in Act 3, Scene 3. Compare this description with a performance of the scene you have seen.

> **So in the midst of the extravagant and irresistible expression of Romeo's grief, at being banished from the object of his love, his voice suddenly stops, and falters, and is choked with sobs of tenderness, when he comes to Juliet's name.**

A 1935 production had the actors playing Romeo and Mercutio swapping roles on alternate nights. As these two actors, John Gielgud and Laurence Olivier, were considered two of the greatest actors of their generation, but also very different in their approaches, there was a heightened sense of competition between the two. Many felt that Gielgud succeeded in speaking the verse more persuasively as Romeo, while Olivier's athleticism made him outstanding as Mercutio.

In 1960, director Franco Zeffirelli (who also directed the 1968 film of the play) aimed for youthfulness and vitality in his production. He cut almost a thousand lines from the text and created a vibrant, lush Italian setting. Some criticized his approach for not taking the verse seriously enough, while others appreciated this more natural, spontaneous acting style.

In 1986, Michael Bogdanov directed a modern-dress production of the play. In this, Tybalt wore a leather jacket, while Romeo committed suicide by injecting himself with a hypodermic needle. This production omitted the reconciliation between the Montagues and Capulets at the end of the play. Instead the Prince read the Prologue as a type of press release while revealing two golden statues of the lovers, emphasizing the **materialism** of society.

**materialism** the desire for money and objects of value

Sian Phillips and Michael Byrne played the star-crossed senior citizens in the Bristol Old Vic production

The Bristol Old Vic produced an unusual version of the play in 2010 when they portrayed Romeo and Juliet as 80-year-olds in a care home, one in a private ward and the other in the NHS wing. The other characters in the play were their children and the staff of the nursing home.

### Activity 8

1. Look back at the different stage productions of Romeo and Juliet described in this section. Rank them in the order in which they appeal to you and explain why.

2. Consider when each production was produced and suggest reasons why the director may have made the choices he did.

## Film versions of the play

*Romeo and Juliet* has proved a popular subject for films, even from the earliest silent films. The demands of filmmaking are different from the stage and directors have to consider how to present their film in order to satisfy cinema audiences. Most productions consider it vital that the lovers are attractive to the audience and that the society in which they live is vividly depicted. Many experiment with editing, re-ordering the text, adding characters and creating visually exciting sequences.

In 1936, George Cukor directed two of the leading actors of the day, Leslie Howard (aged 43) and Norma Shearer (aged 34) in the main roles in what was advertised as 'The Greatest Motion Picture of all Time'. Although nominated for awards and admired for its beautiful costumes and sets, the production was criticized for casting actors who were too old to portray youthful lovers. Care was taken with the speaking of the verse and large crowds of dancers and extras were used to swell the more spectacular action scenes.

The mid-twentieth century interpretation of the balcony scene in the original film of *West Side Story*

In 1961, the musical film *West Side Story* (first a Broadway musical in 1957) adapted Shakespeare's play in a radically different way. A modern-dress production set in New York, it focused on two rival gangs, the Puerto Rican Sharks and the white Jets. Rather than Shakespeare's dialogue, the musical used songs and dance to convey the story of the young lovers, Tony, played by Richard Beymer (aged 22), and Maria, played by Natalie Wood (aged 23). The roles of the adult characters were minimized and the emphasis was on the gang warfare between the groups.

One of the most successful adaptations of the film was Franco Zeffirelli's 1968 film, starring Olivia Hussey (aged 15) and Leonard Whiting (aged 17). Similar to his 1960 stage production, the film is set in Renaissance Italy and was filmed to emphasize the beauty of the lovers and their surroundings. However, almost two-thirds of Shakespeare's lines were cut, as was the death of Paris.

## Activity 9

A problem facing many casting directors is choosing actors who look young enough to play Romeo and Juliet, but who also have the acting skill and experience to handle the demanding emotional range and difficult language of the play. Discuss the ages of the various Romeos and Juliets in different productions and then prepare a speech for or against the following statement: 'When casting the roles of Romeo and Juliet, above all else, it is important that the actors are young.'

Baz Luhrmann's *William Shakespeare's Romeo + Juliet*, made in 1996, was an updated version with a pop and hip-hop soundtrack, references to drug use and a Mercutio who appears in drag. The film is edited in a rapid, pop video style and portrays a violent, gun-toting society, which contrasts with the sensitive young lovers portrayed by Leonardo Dicaprio (aged 22) and Clare Danes (aged 17.) Again, the death of Paris is cut from this adaptation.

An entirely different version of the play is the 2011 British 3D computer-animated film *Gnomeo & Juliet*. In this film, two rival sets of garden gnomes battle while the two young romantic gnomes, voiced by James McAvoy and Emily Blunt, find love to a soundtrack which features the music of Elton John. Unlike the previous adaptations mentioned, this movie ends happily.

## Activity 10

Watch a film adaptation of *Romeo and Juliet*.

1. Select a key scene and make notes on how this is presented. You should comment on the:

   - setting
   - casting
   - acting choices
   - visual images
   - editing
   - soundtrack.

2. Write an analysis of the presentation of this key scene in the adaptation you have watched.

The 2013 film of Romeo and Juliet, directed by Carlo Carlei, was adapted by British writer Julian Fellowes, who is known for his period dramas. This adaptation returned the location to a Renaissance setting. Hailee Steinfeld (aged 15) plays Juliet opposite Douglas Booth (aged 19) as Romeo. The film was described by one of its publicists as 'Romeo and Juliet for the Twilight Generation' and its trailer emphasizes a sense of danger with black cloaks, fire and darkness, ending with the words '#ForbiddenLove.'

Douglas Booth and Hailee Steinfeld play Romeo and Juliet in the 2013 film

## Activity 11

Research two different productions of *Romeo and Juliet* and create a presentation comparing them. You can find many online resources to help you explore different film and stage versions of *Romeo and Juliet*, including video clips, reviews, photo galleries and scholarly articles. Many large theatres have online education packs and information about their past productions.

## Writing about performance

*Upgrade*

Whether or not you are expected to analyse a performance of a Shakespeare play in addition to the text itself, it is vital that you understand that you are writing about a play and how it can be interpreted and performed in order to have the desired impact on an audience. To help when preparing for this aspect of your assessment, consider:

- what performance guidance is contained within the text itself, such as stage directions and characterization
- what are some of the important directorial and acting choices that can be made for this scene/play
- if the question is asking you to think in an original way as a director or if you are being asked to comment on another director's ideas
- what aspects of the scene could be interpreted in more than one way
- how important are the visual elements of the scene
- how the actors use their voices, facial expression and gestures to convey their intentions and emotions
- how costumes and props help to tell the story
- when and where is the production set
- how the editing of the script (e.g. cutting lines, re-ordering scenes, adding or omitting characters or events) shapes the story.

Remember that for the highest grades, examiners are looking for subtle, sophisticated, accurate and detailed points.

It is easy to feel overwhelmed by the demands of an assessment. You may be worried about timing, understanding the question, organizing your ideas or the quality of your writing. It is important to remember that assessments are designed to allow you to demonstrate your skills, not to trick you.

## Preparing for your assessment

If you are sitting an exam on your set text, make sure you have studied at least one actual exam paper beforehand. Often the exam board will have questions for a number of different texts in the same paper (as other schools will have studied different plays and novels), so you should get used to locating quickly the questions you will need to answer.

Take a few minutes to read over all the questions for your text, particularly if you have a choice of which to answer. You might also want to consider the order in which you approach your questions. Some students prefer to answer the questions worth the most marks first, while others start with the easiest questions to gain confidence and then move on. There is no single right way of doing this, but make sure that you are spending an appropriate amount of time given the marks being awarded for each question.

## Understanding the question

Carefully read the question and underline key words, even if you think you have answered a similar question before. Every year, students lose important marks because they have made basic mistakes like writing about the wrong character or scene or misunderstanding the focus of the question.

Here are some typical essay-style questions, with key words and phrases underlined. This is followed by an explanation of what each question requires.

### Characters

> How does Shakespeare present the character of Tybalt in the play?

Usually the character or characters that you are meant to be discuss will be specified in the question. The wording 'Shakespeare presents...' is useful as it will remind you to write about the characters as something constructed by a playwright and not as real people.

> Explore how the attitudes and feelings of Lady Capulet are presented in the play.

'Explore' is a common word in these questions and invites you to write in an imaginative and insightful way. The word 'how' tells you that you should *analyse* the literary techniques used to convey her 'attitudes and feelings' and not just repeat what she says. You should also consider how 'attitudes' might be different from 'feelings'.

> Compare two scenes in which a character behaves in an unexpected way in *Romeo and Juliet*.

The word 'compare' is important here. You should be looking for similarities and differences rather than just writing about two separate scenes. In this specific question, you should use phrases such as 'similarly,' 'both', 'however' or 'unlike the previous scene' to draw out similarities and differences. Think about what 'unexpected' means and make sure you explain why the actions are 'unexpected'.

Remember to choose key moments when the characters reveal their personalities through dialogue and/or action, and what others say about them. Note if the character changes or develops in the course of the play.

## Themes

> Explore how the theme of fate is presented in the play.

This question gives you the opportunity to look not only at how fate is important for the play's plot but also at the literary techniques, such as personification, used to present it to the audience. One of the dangers to avoid with this style of question is the temptation to re-tell the play's story rather than highlighting and analysing key moments.

## Relationships

> Explore what we learn about the relationship between Friar Lawrence and Romeo in Act 2, Scene 3 and one other scene in the play.

Relationship questions allow you to investigate more than one character and to compare and contrast them. You can also consider if the relationship changes or is integral to the play's plot. Carefully choose a contrasting scene to allow you to demonstrate more insight, rather than repeating similar ideas.

## Language

> Comment on how the language in Act 5, Scene 3, lines 12–87 reveals the characters of Romeo and Paris.

Language means not only the words used, but the different literary techniques employed such as metaphors, similes, etc. However, when answering this style of question, you should not just identify literary techniques but analyse what the language used reveals about the characters. The examiner will be looking for you to demonstrate insight.

## Performance

> Explore how the films or plays you have seen portray the character of Prince Escales.

When answering this style of question, make it clear which films or plays you are writing about, for example, by mentioning the director and year in which it was produced. Be careful to avoid the trap of just describing what you have seen. Consider why choices were made and what effects they had on the audience. This gives you the opportunity to demonstrate your knowledge about how this text can be performed either on stage or in a film, and to consider aspects of interpretation.

> Given your understanding of Act 3, Scene 1, explain how the roles of Mercutio and Benvolio could be performed in lines 1–34.

This style of question gives you the opportunity to think as a director and explain how you would guide the performers in order to convey this scene to the audience. Often the best responses are not the flashiest. Instead they are the ones that aim for depth and insight, considering what words might be emphasized, when there might be a turning point in the scene and what facial expressions and gestures could be employed.

## Planning your answer

With the pressure of time, it is tempting to launch into answering the question straightaway. However, good responses are almost always well planned. Sensible planning helps you to avoid repetition and to check that you are meeting the assessment criteria.

There are many different ways of planning and you should choose the one that works best for you. Several techniques are demonstrated below using the question: Explore how the attitudes and feelings of Lady Capulet are presented in the play.

## Spider diagram

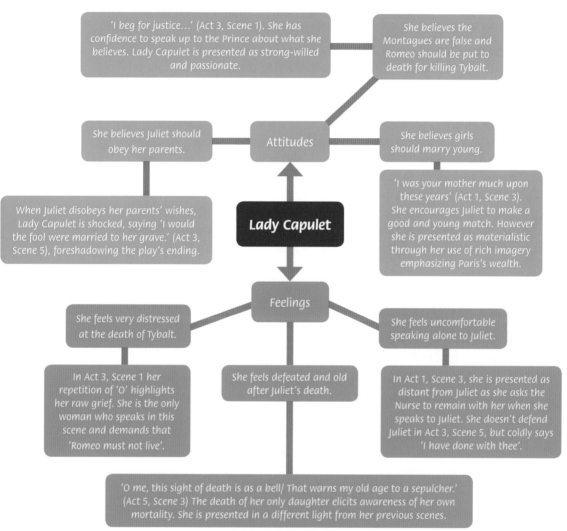

'I beg for justice...' (Act 3, Scene 1). She has confidence to speak up to the Prince about what she believes. Lady Capulet is presented as strong-willed and passionate.

She believes the Montagues are false and Romeo should be put to death for killing Tybalt.

She believes Juliet should obey her parents.

**Attitudes**

She believes girls should marry young.

When Juliet disobeys her parents' wishes, Lady Capulet is shocked, saying 'I would the fool were married to her grave.' (Act 3, Scene 5), foreshadowing the play's ending.

**Lady Capulet**

'I was your mother much upon these years' (Act 1, Scene 3). She encourages Juliet to make a good and young match. However she is presented as materialistic through her use of rich imagery emphasizing Paris's wealth.

**Feelings**

She feels very distressed at the death of Tybalt.

She feels uncomfortable speaking alone to Juliet.

In Act 3, Scene 1 her repetition of 'O' highlights her raw grief. She is the only woman who speaks in this scene and demands that 'Romeo must not live'.

She feels defeated and old after Juliet's death.

In Act 1, Scene 3, she is presented as distant from Juliet as she asks the Nurse to remain with her when she speaks to Juliet. She doesn't defend Juliet in Act 3, Scene 5, but coldly says 'I have done with thee'.

'O me, this sight of death is as a bell/ That warns my old age to a sepulcher.' (Act 5, Scene 3) The death of her only daughter elicits awareness of her own mortality. She is presented in a different light from her previous scenes.

### Tips for assessment

*Upgrade*

If you choose to use a spider diagram to plan your answer in the assessment, don't forget to number your ideas in the order that you wish to discuss them in your essay.

## Paragraphs

You might want to begin by shaping your ideas into paragraphs, for example:

**Paragraph 1** Importance of Lady Capulet's feelings and attitudes towards: her daughter, marriage, grief and revenge in the play. (Show understanding of form and structure.) How is she first presented to the audience and what is her dramatic function in the play?

**Paragraph 2** How her feelings towards Juliet are established. Compare to the Nurse in Act 1, Scene 3. Consider how she is presented as being distant from Juliet, changing her mind from talking in secret to requesting the Nurse to stay. Explore the formality of her language. Desire for Juliet to make an appropriate marriage to a wealthy man rather than considering Juliet's wishes (use of extended metaphor describing Paris, suggesting Paris's wealth and possible reason for her excitement about this match). Subsequent coldness in Act 3, Scene 5 when Juliet disobeys her. (Show understanding of context and language.)

**Paragraph 3** Her feelings and attitude towards Tybalt's death. Explore her emotive language, such as the repetition of 'O' and 'blood'. Family loyalty and distrust of the Montagues. Has confidence to speak out for what she believes (contrast with Lady Montague.) Wants revenge and expresses this in rhyming couplets. (Show understanding of language and plot.)

**Paragraph 4** Feelings upon Juliet's death. Again she uses the exclamation 'O' but the tone is different. Lady Capulet is presented as being more subdued and defeated now. (Show understanding of resolution.)

**Paragraph 5** Conclusion, including different ways Lady Capulet can be interpreted.

Note that in this plan, the student has highlighted opportunities to demonstrate understanding of language, form, structure and context.

# Answering the question

Always try to think ahead before you start writing. Thinking and planning ahead will help you to:

- struture your answer logically
- target the precise demands of the question
- avoid missing out points that are crucial to your argument
- include appropriate quotations.

Plans can take a variety of forms. However, a brief list is often the most helpful as it allows you to put your ideas into a logical sequence. Don't spend more than six or seven minutes on a plan. Jot down your ideas and then start.

You should begin with a short introduction and it is useful to employ some of the wording in the question in your opening paragraph, and elsewhere in your essay, to ensure that you are staying on topic and answering the set question.

Each of your following paragraphs should start with a **topic sentence**, which you will then develop and support with evidence from the text. Make sure that these central paragraphs include well-selected quotations and analysis. One of the most common errors is to lapse into re-telling the plot or describing a scene rather than analysing it, so make sure every paragraph includes ideas, evidence and analysis.

> **topic sentence** the first sentence in a paragraph, which introduces the subject or main ideas that follow

Watch your timing in the exam, especially if there are several questions worth different marks. Also be aware if your exam board rewards contextual knowledge or comparisons. There is no point in giving a detailed analysis of marriage in Shakespeare's time if all the marks are awarded for language, form and structure.

## Using quotations

You will need to support your ideas with evidence from the text. This usually involves selecting a quotation that helps you to make your point and then giving further explanation or analysis. This process is often called PEE, which stands for Point, Evidence, Explanation. An example of this might be:

> **Point** Death is associated with love throughout the play.
>
> **Evidence** In Act 4, Scene 5, Capulet tells Paris that Death has 'lain with thy wife' and in Act 5, Scene 3, Romeo says that 'Death is amorous' to explain why Juliet still looks so beautiful in death.
>
> **Explanation** This use of personification creates an eerie and macabre image, which confirms the 'death-mark'd' quality of the young lovers' passion.

### Activity 1

Choose one of the sample essay questions in this section and write your own Point, Evidence, Explanation (PEE) paragraph. Then try writing a chain of three different PEE responses on the same topic. Check your work to make sure you are making three different points, not just repeating the same idea.

**Tips for assessment**

Remember it is better to use short, well-selected quotations rather than copying out long sections of the play. When using quotations, embed them into your writing in a grammatically correct way, as demonstrated in the example on the previous page, rather than setting them out separately.

# Sample questions

**1**

**a)** Write about the way Shakespeare presents the feud between the families in this extract from Act 1, Scene 1.

| | |
|---|---|
| **Tybalt** | What, drawn and talk of peace! I hate the word, |
| | As I hate hell, all Montagues, and thee. |
| | Have at thee, coward. |

*They fight*

*Enter, several of both houses, who join the fray, and three or four* Citizens *as* Officers *of the Watch, with clubs or partisans*

| | |
|---|---|
| **Officers** | Clubs, bills, and partisans! Strike! Beat them down! |
| | Down with the Capulets! Down with the Montagues! |

*Enter old* Capulet *in his gown, and his wife* Lady Capulet

| | |
|---|---|
| **Capulet** | What noise is this? Give me my long sword, ho! |
| **Lady Capulet** | A crutch, a crutch! why call you for a sword? |
| **Capulet** | My sword, I say! old Montague is come, |
| | And flourishes his blade in spite of me. |

*Enter old* Montague *and his wife* Lady Montague

| | |
|---|---|
| **Montague** | Thou villain Capulet! – Hold me not, let me go. |
| **Lady Montague** | Thou shalt not stir one foot to seek a foe. |

*Enter* Prince Escales *with his train*

| | |
|---|---|
| **Prince** | Rebellious subjects, enemies to peace, |
| | Profaners of this neighbour-stained steel – |
| | Will they not hear? – What, ho! you men, you beasts! |
| | That quench the fire of your pernicious rage |
| | With purple fountains issuing from your veins: |
| | On pain of torture, from those bloody hands |
| | Throw your mistemper'd weapons to the ground, |
| | And hear the sentence of your moved prince. |

**b)** Write about the ways Shakespeare presents this feud in a different part of the play.

**2**

Compare how Shakespeare presents the relationship between Juliet and her Nurse in the following extract from Act 2, Scene 5 (lines 29–47) and another section of the play.

**3**

Given your understanding of the roles of Capulet and Tybalt, explain how you believe the actors should perform Act 1, Scene 5, lines 53–91. Consider their use of movement, voice, facial expression and gesture.

**4**

Compare the presentation of Friar Lawrence in the text of *Romeo and Juliet* with the presentation of Friar Lawrence in the Baz Luhrmann film *William Shakespeare's Romeo + Juliet*. Use examples from both the play and the film in your response.

**5**

Examine the ways Shakespeare presents the relationship between parents and children in *Romeo and Juliet*.

**6**

Remind yourself of Act 1, Scene 4 and Act 3, Scene 1 in the text and watch the scenes in one or two stage or film versions, or listen to one or two audio versions. By referring closely to Shakespeare's text, explore how the films or plays you have watched or heard portray the character of Mercutio.
You should consider:
• the language he uses to express his thoughts and feelings
• the way other characters react to him
• the dramatic effect of these scenes and their implications for the rest of the play.

**7**

Compare the presentation of the balcony scene in Act 2, Scene 2 in the text of *Romeo and Juliet* with that in your chosen adaptation of the play.

**8**

To what extent does Romeo grow and change as a character in the play. Consider:
• his relationships with his parents and friends
• his attitude towards love
• his actions in Act 5.

# Sample answers

## Sample answer 1

Read the extract below taken from a student response, together with examiner comments, to the following sample question:

> How does Shakespeare present the relationship between Romeo and Mercutio in the play?

At first glance, Romeo and Mercutio may seem to be very different characters as Romeo is the classic lover while Mercutio is a joker. In Act 1, Scene 4, Romeo is still suffering from his unrequited love for Rosaline and does not want to attend the Capulet party, but Mercutio is in lively, high spirits. By presenting these contrasting moods, Romeo is singled out as being different from his friends. However, a sign of their friendship is their ability to pun with each other, such as Romeo's suggestion that Mercutio has 'nimble soles' while he has a 'soul of lead'. This word play also highlights their opposing moods. Mercutio is confident enough to tease the romantic Romeo by saying 'that dreamers often lie'. He does not take seriously Romeo's sadness over Rosaline, perhaps because he has a different view of love. Mercutio's Queen Mab speech is unlike any of Romeo's speeches in the play. Such is Mercutio's imagination, it is as if he could continue this fantastical speech until he is interrupted by Romeo saying 'thou talk'st of nothing'. This seems to suggest that Romeo has entered a more serious phase while his friends are still happy to riddle and joke. However Romeo is persuaded by Mercutio and Benvolio to attend the party which will change his life forever.

Romeo and Mercutio speak in very different ways about love. Mercutio has a more irreverent and aggressive attitude towards love, saying, 'If love be rough with you, be rough with love', while Romeo claims 'under love's heavy burden do I sink'. It may be that they feel differently about it because Mercutio has never really experienced love, as Romeo says that Mercutio 'jests at scars that never felt a wound'. Shakespeare highlights the contrast between these two characters by having some of Mercutio's rudest jokes ('thou a pop'rin pear') followed shortly by one of the most romantic scenes in literature, the balcony scene.

Shows knowledge of the characters, but must remember to focus on their relationship.

Good examples of word play and suggestion of meaning and effect.

Contrasts characters but needs to consider relationship more.

Makes interesting point on structure, but could comment more on language.

In Act 2, Scene 4, we see Mercutio and Romeo have a contest of wits where they are punning with each other. In this scene, Romeo is happy, probably because he is hopeful that he and Juliet will wed soon. However, Mercutio endangers Romeo's learning of the vital news from the Nurse by his rudeness in calling her a 'bawd'. Shakespeare contrasts Romeo's behaviour in this scene by his far more polite behaviour to the woman he calls 'Nurse' and the way he speaks to her, which she describes as 'gentleman-like'. In this scene, Romeo rejects Mercutio's behaviour and establishes Juliet as his priority.

In Act 3, Scene 1, we see a different side to the relationship between Mercutio and Romeo. Both are in very different moods at the beginning of the scene with Mercutio wanting to fight and Romeo, having just married Juliet, feeling more peaceful. As Romeo has not confided in him, Mercutio does not understand what Romeo considers to be a 'vile submission' and feels that he must, for honour's sake, fight Tybalt. It is ironic that by trying to avoid bloodshed, Romeo causes it by standing between Mercutio and Tybalt, allowing Tybalt to mortally wound Mercutio. Shakespeare presents Mercutio as being as angry with Romeo as well as Tybalt when he curses both the Montague and Capulet houses ('a plague a'both houses!') which makes Romeo feel guilty for his role in Mercutio's death.

Shakespeare makes clear Romeo's great affection for Mercutio when he calls him his 'very' (meaning 'true') friend and determines to seek revenge for his death. He also speaks his only words of criticism about Juliet in saying that she has made him 'effeminate', emphasizing the importance of Mercutio to him. Despite their many differences, this is a point where Romeo becomes more like Mercutio as, without thinking of the consequences, he throws himself into action against Tybalt. He is willing to die for Mercutio's sake, saying, 'Either thou or I, or both, must go with him'. His actions at this point lead to his banishment and the ultimate tragedy of the play.

Although Mercutio's role in the play is not as large as Romeo's, he is important in showing Romeo's friendships and also in being the catalyst for the play's tragedy.

**Locates a key moment in their relationship.**

**Uses word 'relationship' to ensure staying on topic.**

**Understands plot and irony.**

**Notes transition in Romeo's feelings and turning point in the plot.**

This is a strong response which considers many key moments in the play involving Romeo and Mercutio. There are short well-selected quotations to support ideas. Turning points in the relationship are identified. It is important to maintain the focus on the relationship, however, perhaps by contrasting it with other relationships.

## Sample answer 2

Read the extract below taken from a student response, together with examiner comments, to the following sample question:

> Given your understanding of the character of Juliet, explain how you would have an actor perform Act 4, Scene 3.

In my production of the play, I would like the actor playing Juliet to highlight her panic and isolation in this scene. When she speaks to her Nurse at the beginning of the scene, it is important that the audience sees that she is trying to behave as if she still trusts the Nurse. The Nurse might be undertaking some action which we have seen her do previously in the play, like brushing Juliet's hair. However, on the line 'leave me', Juliet might gently push the Nurse from her, so that the Nurse has little choice but to go.

*Thinks like a director from the very beginning.*

When Lady Capulet enters, there should be a certain coldness in their exchange of dialogue, but still polite so as not to raise any suspicions. Juliet refers to this 'sudden business', which suggests that it is not a joyful event and that Lady Capulet has her 'hands full all' might also mean that this is more Lady Capulet's event than Juliet's. The Nurse is unusually quiet in this scene, so perhaps she senses that she has displeased Juliet. Just before she leaves the room, she and Juliet could exchange a last glance reminding the audience of their former closeness.

*Shows insight into characters.*

There should be a clear transition when Lady Capulet and the Nurse leave as Juliet can now stop pretending to be the obedient daughter. I think she should stand up and move in a more agitated way. She might run to the door on the line, 'I'll call them back again to comfort me' and begin to shout for the Nurse, then stop herself. There should be a change in her facial expression when she says, 'my dismal scene I needs must act alone', showing that she can no longer depend on anyone else and her voice should be empty and mournful. As the iambic pentameter line is incomplete on 'Come, vial', I think this means that there can be a few seconds of silence while Juliet goes to fetch the vial. I think this should be hidden under her pillow and she should hold it up to the light and look at it with wonder and fear.

*Spots transitions and makes insightful point.*

*Makes useful point about using the metre of the verse.*

Imaginative ideas, but could consider the effect of these actions.

There is another change when Juliet begins to worry that the Friar has tricked her, but she should reassure herself on the line, 'For he hath still been tried a holy man.' When she begins to imagine that she might wake in the tomb, I would have her sit on the bed and imagine that it was the tomb. On the words 'terror of the place', her eyes should grow wide and she should imagine that her 'buried ancestors' are beginning to emerge around her. She might throw out an arm as if fighting off the evil spirits she imagines in the tomb and her voice should be shrill on phrases like 'shrieks like mandrakes' torn out of the earth'.

Makes point on the structure.

The speech should reach its climax on 'Stay, Tybalt, stay!'. At this point, Juliet could jump off the bed and move as if she were protecting Romeo from Tybalt. Saying 'Seeking out Romeo' reminds Juliet that Romeo is most important thing in the world to her and this gives her the strength to drink the potion. When she says 'Romeo' three times, I think she should say it three different ways: the first time as if she is remembering him as if he needs to be protected; the second time showing how much she loves him and the last time bravely to give herself the strength to drink.

This is detailed and sophisticated.

Conclusion feels a little rushed and unsupported compared to the rest of the answer.

At the end of the scene I would have Juliet hold up the potion as if toasting to Romeo and then drinking it as quickly as possible before she can change her mind. I would then have her curl up on the bed, like a baby.

This candidate makes it very clear from the start that she is thinking of practical ways of expressing her ideas about the scene in detail.

# Sample answer 3

Read the extract below taken from a student response, together with examiner comments, to the following sample question:

> Compare the presentation of the theme of violence in Act 1, Scene 1 in the play *Romeo and Juliet* and the Baz Luhrmann film *William Shakespeare's Romeo + Juliet*.

I think the movie directed by Baz Luhrmann is better than the play because it is more exciting and easier to understand. For example, it comes up on the screen who the characters are and if they are a Montague or a Capulet, but that can be confusing in the play. The movie also dresses the Montagues and the Capulets differently, with the Montagues wearing Hawaiian-type shirts and the Capulets sharper outfits.

*This is not a strong beginning and needs to focus on the theme of violence.*

There is a lot of violence in both, but it is more frightening in the movie because they use guns (even though they say things like 'put up your swords' which is what is engraved on the guns). The movie has been updated so that there are guns and cars. On the car licence plates, it says 'Mon' or 'Cap' to show which side they belong to. They have also chopped up the lines, for example, they start with 'A dog of the house of Capulet moves me' (changed from 'Montague' in the play). Also one of the characters repeats the line 'I am a pretty piece of flesh.'

*Notes that the movie has been updated, which is an important comparison.*

*Avoid ending with 'hanging quotations'; they need to be followed by analysis.*

My favourite character is Tybalt and he is clearly a violent character. We are introduced to him by seeing his silver heels, which seem dangerous. He puts out a small cigar with his heel and then goes away. When he returns there is another close-up of the silver heels of his shoes and then he lights up a small cigar. Even though others seem frightened, he looks, in close-up, cold and calm. I think this shows that he is a character who enjoys violence. When he shoots one of the Montague characters, he has a little smile on his face.

*This is too descriptive and loses focus on the theme.*

*Makes a valid comparison but should tie in more with the theme of violence.*

There is comedy in both the script and the film. In the play, it comes from the characters deciding whether or not they can 'bite their thumbs' at each other, whereas in the film, it comes more from the reactions of characters like the nuns and the lady who hits a character with her handbag. The 'biting thumb' section of the film is more frightening, as the Montague boys' voices sound more scared. Abram, the Capulet man has already suddenly stopped his car and seems like he is going to fight.

Attempts insight into character, but needs to compare with the play text.

The actual fight is edited in a very exciting way, with lots of quick shots. Early on both Tybalt and Benvolio are shown in close-up and Benvolio looks much more frightened than Tybalt. When Tybalt hears a noise he quickly turns around and almost shoots a little boy, but instead of saying 'sorry' just says 'bang', showing that he doesn't take anything seriously. Because they are using guns rather than swords, it seems like the characters are more in danger of being killed, which also makes it more exciting. Some sections are speeded up and some, like Tybalt flying through the air, are done in slow motion. This makes it a very unpredictable scene.

Makes comparison but should draw out more meaning from this.

As the scene has been updated, there is a greater variety of violence like the petrol which can cause a fire or the cars which can cause an accident. There are also a lot of bystanders who could also be hurt. In the play, it says that others 'join the fray' but we don't know if there are children or women present as there are in the film.

The soundtrack of the film also adds to the theme of violence because there is a lot of screaming and shouting. It starts with a rock-type song at the beginning but ends with a classical song and the sound of a police helicopter. One section, with the creaking sign, is very quiet, but that just makes it more exciting when Tybalt enters and everyone begins to fight.

This is descriptive and does not compare with play.

In a high-angle shot from the helicopter, it seems like the whole city of Verona Beach is at war as you can see lots of violence and scenes of destruction. Benvolio and Tybalt look ready to shoot each other but then drop their guns in slow motion at the order of the Prince.

Although this candidate has clearly enjoyed the film, too frequently he forgets to compare it with the play. There should be a balance in writing about the play and the film. Details from the movie are noted, but appropriate explanations are not always present.

## Sample answer 4

Read the extract below taken from a student response, together with examiner comments, to the following sample question:

> Explore the use of language in Act 2, Scene 2 of *Romeo and Juliet*.

Act 2, Scene 2 is one of the most romantic scenes in the play and Shakespeare uses many poetic techniques such as personification and nature imagery to present the love between the characters. It is also important that this scene happens at night and that there is a sense of danger should the lovers be discovered.

*Immediately suggests knowledge of some language points.*

Nature imagery is used in Romeo's opening soliloquy. He says that Juliet is 'the sun', which makes her seem bright and powerful. He contrasts her with the 'envious moon', which is an example of personification. Throughout the play there are contrasts between light and dark, and this is another example, but it is also an example of exaggeration because he is giving Juliet qualities she couldn't possibly possess. This shows Romeo's romantic nature. Much of the imagery he uses associates her with heaven: 'fairest stars', 'eyes in heaven', 'dear saint,' 'bright angel'. These are all examples of Romeo putting Juliet above himself, as she is literally when she appears on the balcony.

*Uses terms like 'personification' correctly and makes interesting point about Juliet being above Romeo.*

Both Romeo and Juliet speak about parts of the body. Romeo compares Juliet's eyes to stars and wishes that he could be a glove so that he could 'touch that cheek'. Juliet wonders what a Montague is, deciding it is not a 'hand nor foot...' and makes what some think could be a rude joke by saying 'nor any other part/ Belonging to a man'. This emphasizes the physical attraction between the characters.

In some ways, Juliet's language is more practical and down-to-earth than Romeo's. When he makes bold, flowery vows to the moon, she tells him not to, but to swear only 'by thy gracious self'. She seems to want to avoid the games of being in love, but just to enjoy how deep and sudden this realization is. Romeo's use of poetry has developed, however, from the clichéd oxymorons that he used to describe Rosaline in Act 1, Scene 1 to his passionate declarations to Juliet.

*This is a slightly under-developed paragraph and needs more evidence.*

This scene, like most in the play, is written in blank verse, but there are a few instances of rhyming. Juliet uses the rhyming

Discusses rhyme with insight.

couplets of 'rest/breast', which signals the first time she tries to say goodbye to Romeo and again there is a rhyming couplet on 'adieu' and 'true'. The rhyming couplets are like false exits and the lovers keep returning to each other. At the end of the scene Juliet leaves with a rhyming couplet of 'sorrow' and 'morrow', and Romeo completes his speech with two rhyming couplets, finally ensuring that they depart separately and the scene ends.

Identifies iambic pentameter, but struggles a little with analysis.

There are instances of interrupted or shared iambic lines when the Nurse calls to interrupt them and when Romeo and Juliet share some snatched lines, which suggests that these might be said in a quick and breathless way.

Uses the term correctly and shows understanding of the play.

Juliet foreshadows the ending of the play with her ominous realization that their relationship is 'too rash, too unadvis'd, too sudden'. Romeo seems more impulsive and less inclined to think of the future. It is Juliet who wonders if his love is 'honourable' and his 'purpose marriage'. This is another example of her thinking in a more practical way. She also seems more aware of the dangers of this encounter. On one hand, she worries that her kinsmen 'will murder thee' and on the other, she worries that Romeo 'mayst prove false'. Because she has been overheard declaring her love for him, she knows that there is no point in 'coying to be strange'. Her words convey her conflicting joy combining embarrassment and fear at suddenly finding herself in love.

Includes a PEE paragraph.

The bond between the couple is evident in the falconry/bird imagery towards the end of the scene, which suggests that Juliet wishes she had the control over Romeo that a falconer has over his hawk. But more ominously she also says that if he were her bird, 'I should kill thee with much cherishing'. This is one of many instances in the play when love and death are joined and foreshadow the ending.

Makes a short conclusion with a little repetition, but sums up the points.

The language in this scene highlights the intensity of the emotions of characters experiencing their first mutual love, but also hints at the dangers that await them.

This is a confident response, showing an impressive understanding of a number of language points such as personification and rhyme. A few paragraphs are under-developed and techniques like repetition could have been considered. The candidate demonstrates insight into the scene and the play.

# Glossary

**antagonist** a character who opposes the protagonist

**archaic** very old and no longer in use

**bawdy** coarse, rude, lewd

**bear-baiting** a popular Elizabethan sport where hunting dogs attacked a chained bear, usually resulting in the death of many of the animals involved

**blank verse** unrhymed lines of poetry with a regular metre

**catharsis** the purification or cleansing of emotion

**Chorus** in Elizabethan drama, an actor who recites the Prologue and may comment at other times on the action of the play

**clichéd** unoriginal and over-used

**confidante** someone to whom secrets are confided

**coup de foudre** an amazing or unusually quick and dramatic occurrence; from the French meaning 'a lightning flash'

**deus ex machina** a dramatic term for an unlikely solution to a plot dilemma by the sudden introduction of a new character, event or object such as the Friar's sleeping potion

**dramatic irony** when the words or action of a scene are understood by the audience but not by one or more of the characters on stage. For example, when Juliet says 'Ay, madam, from the reach of my hands/Would none but I might venge my cousin's death', her mother believes that Juliet wishes she could kill Romeo, whereas the audience understands that she wishes to protect him

**extended metaphor** a metaphor which is developed for several lines or more

**foreshadowing** a literary device in which the author hints at what will happen at a later point

**hay** a stab to the heart, possibly fatal as it derives from the Italian *hai* meaning 'you have it'

**hierarchy** a system in which there is a clear ranking of groups or individuals, some having more power and status than others

**iambic pentameter** a line of verse with ten syllables, forming five 'feet', where the stress falls on the second syllable in each foot, e.g. 'di dum' as in 'He jests at scars that never felt a wound.' (Act 2, Scene 2)

**imagery** the use of visual or other vivid language to convey ideas or emotions

**innuendo** a hint or hidden reference to something rude, often sexual

**leading man** the actor playing the main role, often one of romantic interest

**materialism** the desire for money and objects of value

**metaphor** a figure of speech applied to something to suggest a resemblance, without using the words 'like' or 'as'

**oxymoron** a figure of speech in which two contradictory or extremely unlikely ideas or images are joined

**parody** to mock or make fun of something by imitating it

**passado** a manoeuvre in which a sword is thrust forward and one foot advanced at the same time

**pathos** something that creates feelings of sympathy and pity

**patriarchy** a community or society in which men are dominant and hold the power

**personification** when human qualities are given to something non-human, such as an object or an idea

**plague** the Bubonic Plague or 'Black Death', a deadly infectious disease which was rapidly spread by infected people and animals

**Prologue** in drama, an introductory scene, often written in verse, which establishes the themes, plot or characters of the play; from the Greek *pro* (before) and *logos* (word)

**prose** any writing in continuous form without rhythm or rhyme

**protagonist** the main character

**pun** a type of joke or word play that relies on the similar sound but different meaning of words

**punto reverso** the left-to-right cut of a sword

**Puritans** a group of strict English Protestants who were against social pleasures such as the theatre, which they thought were an encouragement to vice

**reciprocate** to give something (e.g. love) in return; opposite of unrequited

**rhyming couplet** two consecutive lines which rhyme

**ribald** crude or vulgar humour, usually involving jokes about sex

**ribaldry** crude talk or behaviour

**soliloquy** where a character voices aloud their innermost thoughts for the audience to hear

**sonnet** a 14-line poem with a formal rhyme scheme and condensed form; often for expressing strong emotions, particularly love; in Shakespearean sonnets the rhyme scheme is ABABCDCDEFEFGG

**theme** a subject or idea that is repeated or developed in a literary work

**topic sentence** the first sentence in a paragraph, which introduces the subject or main ideas that follow

**tour de force** a performance requiring great skill that attracts admiration from the audience

**tragedy** a play in which the main character, usually a man of high status, is brought down through a combination of his own personal weaknesses and factors beyond his control, such as fate

**tragic flaw** a defect or failing in the tragic protagonist that brings around his downfall, e.g. Macbeth's ambition or Othello's jealousy

**unrequited love** unreturned love, where the person who is in love is not loved in return by the object of their affection

**vitality** vigour and energy

# OXFORD
UNIVERSITY PRESS

Great Clarendon Street, Oxford, OX2 6DP,

United Kingdom

Oxford University Press is a department of the University of Oxford.

It furthers the University's objective of excellence in research, scholarship, and education by publishing worldwide. Oxford is a registered trade mark of Oxford University Press in the UK and in certain other countries

British Library Cataloguing in Publication Data

Data available

ISBN 978-0-19-830481-4

10 9 8 7 6 5 4 3 2 1

MIX
Paper from
responsible sources
FSC® C007785

Printed in Great Britain by Bell and Bain Ltd., Glasgow

### Acknowledgements

**Cover:** Konstanttin/Shutterstock

Photos: **p.7:** Igor Bulgarin/Shutterstock; **p.9:** Pictorial Press Ltd/ Alamy; **p.13:** AF archive/Alamy; **p.17:** Photostage; **p.21:** Moviestore collection Ltd/Alamy; **p.25:** Image provided courtesy of Houston Ballet, Ballet: Romeo and Juliet, Dancer(s) Karina Gonzalez and Joseph Walsh, Photo by Amitava Sarkar; **p.28:** GL Archive/Alamy; **p.30:** Pictorial Press Ltd/Alamy; **p.32:** SSPL via Getty Images; **p.36:** AF archive/Alamy; **p.40:** Photostage; **p.43:** Moviestore collection Ltd/Alamy; **p.46:** Photostage; **p.54:** Pictorial Press Ltd/Alamy; **p.58:** Mary Evans Picture Library/Alamy; **p.61:** imagebroker/Alamy; **p.68:** travelibUK/Alamy; **p.73:** Photostage; **p.74:** Pictorial Press Ltd/Alamy; **p.76:** Pictorial Press Ltd/Alamy;

We are grateful to the following for permission to reproduce copyright material:

Extract from *Elizabeth's London: Everyday life in Elizabethan London* by Liza Picard Phoenix, 2004), copyright © Liza Picard 2003, reprinted by permission of The Orion Publishing Group, London.

Extract from *Tragedy: A Very Short Introduction* by Adrian Poole (OUP, 2005), reprinted by permission of Oxford University Press.

We have tried to trace and contact all copyright holders before publication. If notified, the publishers will be pleased to rectify any errors or omissions at the earliest opportunity.